Lead with Energy and
Create Ripples of Impact

KAFI LONDON

Copyright © 2025 Kafi London

All rights reserved. No part of this publication may be reproduced, distributed, or transmitted in any form or by any means, including photocopying, recording, or other electronic or mechanical methods, without the prior written permission of the publisher, except in the case of brief quotations embodied in critical reviews and certain other noncommercial uses permitted by copyright law.

Every effort has been made to trace and seek permission for the use of the original source material used within this book. Where the attempt has been unsuccessful, the publisher would be pleased to hear from the author/publisher to rectify any omission.

First published in 2025 by Hambone Publishing
www.hambonepublishing.com.au

Editing by Emily Stephenson, Mish Phillips and Felicity Harrison
Interior design by David W. Edelstein
Author's picture by Qiana Avery

For information about this title, contact:
Kafi London
hello@kafilondon.com
KafiLondon.com

ISBN 978-1-922357-80-9 (paperback)
ISBN 978-1-922357-81-6 (ebook)
ISBN 978-1-922357-82-3 (audiobook)

*To all those who find their light dimming,
here's to reigniting it and
sending good vibes out into the world.*

Contents

Introduction 1
    From Pedals to People Power 6
    How this book will help you.................................. 7

PART I: WHY PERSON-TO-PEOPLE ENERGY MATTERS

Chapter 1: Energy Is Everything 15
    What does energetic leadership look like? 16
    Why aren't we leading with energy already? 18
    How your energy impacts others 21
    Key Takeaways.. 27
    Vibe Shifters... 28

Chapter 2: The Transfer of Energy 29
    Energy as currency 29
    From sunshine to synergy 32
    Key Takeaways.. 33
    Vibe Shifters... 34

Chapter 3: The Ripple Effect 35
    Understanding the ripple effect 36
    Rippling examples 36
    Amani's superpowers 40
    How ripples turn into waves 46
    Key Takeaways.. 48
    Vibe Shifters... 49

PART II: HOW TO LEAD WITH ENERGY

Chapter 4: The Fired Up! Framework 53

Chapter 5: Tune Up 57
    Sparkability Factor 58
    Vitality 60
    Vibe 74
    Value 82
    Voice 91
    Visibility 97
    Key Takeaways 102
    Vibe Shifters 104

Chapter 6: Sync Up 107
    Setting yourself up for success 110
    Decoding cues 114
    Key Takeaways 117
    Vibe Shifters 118

Chapter 7: Lift Up 119
    Lessons from improv 120
    Group gatherings 122
    Lift others your own way 125
    Who are you lifting up? 127
    The Energy Equation 130
    Key Takeaways 141
    Vibe Shifters 142

PART III: ENERGY IN ACTION

Chapter 8: Energyship **145**
   Start the ripple 145
   Ignite Synergy. 147
   Collective Effervescence 147

How can I help? **151**

Let's stay connected **155**

About the Author **157**

Gratitude **159**

Endnotes **163**

Books Referenced **165**

Introduction

"I have learned that people will forget what you said, people will forget what you did, but people will never forget how you made them feel."

- MAYA ANGELOU[1]

The alarm's ascending chime jolts me from a deep slumber.

I'm three snooze buttons in and trying to come to terms with the reality of the situation: I need to get my Black butt out of bed before the dreaded back-up alarm starts screaming at me from out of arm's reach.

Three... two... one... and I'm up!

Getting me out of bed is always a team effort. I partner with my Echo Dot and its voice assistant, Alexa, to kickstart my morning routine. We don't always see eye-to-eye on the issue of how long I deserve to snooze, but we can usually find a suitable compromise. Once I'm up, Alexa rewards me with the date, time, weather, and a list of what's on my calendar that day.

My foggy brain starts to clear as Alexa kicks off a preselected favorite morning song, 'Lovely Day' by Bill Withers. I love this song because it always sets the tone of my day.

I have the next twenty minutes down to a science.

In the two minutes it takes for the shower to heat up, I brush my teeth.

I take a quick shower to wake my body up, dry off, lather myself in body lotion, and put on the workout clothes I laid out the night before.

This all happens on autopilot while my brain focuses on more important things, like re-listening to the playlist of songs I carefully prepared the night before for my 6 a.m. spin class. Over the years, I've learned to listen beyond the lyrics and master the rhythm, cadence, beat drops, and changes in tempo and mood—all elements that help me transform an average riding class into an energizing, energetic experience.

By 05:02, I'm in my car heading to CycleBar East Cobb. Twenty minutes later, I pull into my regular spot and walk the few yards to the front door of the studio, embracing the peace and hush of the early morning.

After fumbling with the various locks, I am alone in a dimly lit room. To my right, thirty-two bikes stand in silent anticipation, waiting for their riders. To my left, a single bike perches on a slightly elevated stage, waiting for me.

I head left to carry out my usual pre-class checklist. As I finish adjusting my bike, Kirstin pops her head in to say a quick *Hi* and lets me know she is all set up to welcome and check-in today's riders.

Glenn, Adam, Melissa, Eric, and Mary arrive like clockwork at

INTRODUCTION

05:45. We say our good mornings and exchange friendly words while respecting each other's energetic boundaries at this early hour.

I play background music to create ambiance and get everyone in the mood as more riders spill in, including other 6 a.m. regulars– Hollis, Lisa, Megan, Mike, and Carolyn who slide in just before I close the studio doors.

It's 05:58. I flip my microphone from off to on.

"Good morning, all! We are starting in less than two minutes. Shake off the cobwebs, and let's make this day count!"

I mount my bike, clip in, and take a micro-moment to inhale sharply and connect with my breath. This simple practice gets me out of my head and into my body. Simultaneously, I scan from rider to rider, picking up subtle cues that provide the insight I need to tailor today's experience.

The energy in the room tells me a lot. The regulars are chatting with each other as they warm up on their bikes, so I know they are up for a challenge. There are also a handful of new riders who look a little hesitant. I make a mental note to adjust my coaching style to create an experience that connects and challenges everyone.

I'm ready to start.

The cool, stale air of the studio fills my lungs. I press play on the instructor's console, turn up the volume, and together we ride to my carefully curated playlist.

As the first song fills the room, I embody my bad-ass instructor alter ego – just like Beyoncé becomes Sasha Fierce on stage, I embrace the energetic responsibility of the experience about to unfold.

When my mic is on, I'm in the zone. Or, as Joel Bauer, a former mentor, would say, I'm *in-state*.

"Alright, beautiful souls, it's time to wake up our bodies and give ourselves the gift of good health today! Let's focus on shifting our energy over the next forty-five minutes as we embrace our time together. Congratulations on making it here this morning. Let's. Do. This!"

Together, we start peddling, each with our own unique mix of dread and excitement. Everyone's wearing a similar look, the one that says, "I want those endorphins... but do I *really* have to sweat this early?"

I guide the riders to adjust their resistance from easy to moderate and settle in on a cadence of 90 to 95 revolutions per minute, which aligns with the tempo of the music.

As time passes, each song brings a new challenge and a new emotion, pushing us further and deeper into the ride. We climb imaginary hills, sprint down virtual roads, and coast along breezy pathways.

As the pace picks up, I watch sleepy expressions give way to focus and determination as the juices start flowing. Together, we ride. It's a symphony of synchronized movement: pedals turning, heartbeats racing, and the occasional I-can't-believe-I'm-doing-this grunt. I keep a keen eye on the room to ensure everyone is aligned with the rhythm of the music.

When we ride as one, it always feels like you can reach out and touch the energy in the room.

INTRODUCTION

Watching each rider push past their limits with commitment and determination always blows my mind. It doesn't matter that they are riding stationary bikes in a dark room at silly-o-clock in the morning, going absolutely nowhere – what matters is the magic of seeing a room full of riders moving in perfect rhythm, responding to my words and the music's tempo.

As the energy in the room builds, there is a collective sense that we are nearing the end. We transition to the final song. Just when everyone is about to tap out, I invite them to lean in and embrace a four-minute sprint to the imaginary finish line.

"Alright team, we're almost there. Four minutes to go!"

"I know you're tired, but this is where we push through and finish strong. As we're in this together, no rider will be left behind."

"Find a pace with moderate intensity you can maintain for the next four minutes. I know we can do this!"

The song picks up; our legs move faster and our determination matches the steady, powerful beat.

"We have got this! Stay strong, stay focused!" I encourage the room, keeping one eye on the clock and the other on the riders.

We sweat through another minute.

"We're halfway there; stay in the game; we've got you!"

The intensity is palpable, a collective energetic force driving everyone forward.

With the imaginary finish line in sight, I call out 20 seconds to go.

The room pulses with perseverance as every rider gives their all. We're united in the final push.

"Three... two... one...nice job. We did it! Congratulations!"

As the cool-down song signals the end of the 45-minute experience, the room fills with relieved exhales and an unmistakable sense of achievement.

We've done it together. We're physically exhausted and mentally invigorated.

As we begin the cool-down, I lead a series of stretches, helping everyone ease out of the ride's intensity. When I reveal the leaderboard, eyes glance up to see where they placed. Sweat drips, chests heave, and the panting subsides. More than anything, eyes shine.

That glow, my friends, is the real magic. It's the culmination of shared energy and collective effort. It's undeniable proof that together, we can light up the world (or at least a dimly lit cycling studio at the crack of dawn). It's what this book will grant you access to.

From Pedals to People Power

It's all about getting fired up – a process less about the physical fuel needed and more about the invisible exchange that makes the magic happen.

Through deliberate guidance, I transfer my energy to others; in turn, they respond with effort and enthusiasm, which I then react to. The exchange ebbs and flows continuously throughout our time together, creating a collective spirit that amplifies the shared experience. This is leading with energy.

INTRODUCTION

Energetic leadership doesn't stop there, though. Sure, I may have facilitated the initial inspiration and motivation this morning, but each rider now takes that energy with them. Whether they know it or not, they'll sprinkle a little of the collective-born determination, resilience, and positivity throughout their day, passing it on to others, who will, in turn, share it with those around them. Before we know it, the energy we co-created in that stuffy little studio ripples across the planet (maybe lighting up the world wasn't such a stretch, after all).

With each pedal stroke and beat of the music, we were not just getting fired up to be excited or get some exercise. We were not only creating collective energy to amplify our riding experience. We were becoming catalysts, kicking off chain reactions of energy that would touch countless others. That was the true power of energetic leadership.

After more than three decades in the people game (and leading over 2,500 spin classes), I've seen how important energy is – especially when it comes to professional success. People buy your energy before they invest in your ideas, goods, or services.

How this book will help you

Energy takes many forms; it might fuel your creativity, help you tackle obstacles head-on, or aid your mental health and resilience. It might also enable you to connect more easily with others, keep you motivated, or help you achieve your goals. It might just do all of the above.

But there is more to the energy game than personal improvement. In fact, focusing energetic exchanges solely on our own individual success is kind of a waste. Yes, there are many personal benefits to energetic wealth that impact the individual, but the real juice is in the catalytic power of the individual. By leading with energy, we create ripples of positivity that impact countless other individuals, groups, and teams.

Through *Fired Up!*, I will help you to:

- Take your energy to the next level (from how you fuel up, share your message and show up)
- Pick up on subtle cues in the room to make sure your message lands every time
- Use practical techniques to shift and lift the vibe of people you connect with.

In **Part 1** we'll look at why person-to-people energy matters and explore its extensive resonating impact.

In **Part 2**, we'll explore how to lead with energy in more detail. We'll look at the Fired Up! Framework and your Sparkability Factor: a guide to help you optimize the different elements of your energy so you are prepared to be a catalyst that ignites others. We'll also discuss how to decode cues to assess the energy of others and then leverage your energy to connect, engage, lift, and leave an impact.

In **Part 3**, we'll bring it all together and take a look at what the result of leading with energy could look like for you. We'll also take a peek at your ripple of impact when you transform people power into an ocean of shared energy and unity known as *Collective Synergy and Collective Effervescence*.

Like most rockstars who lead others, I suspect you are juggling many decisions, dilemmas and demands throughout your day and

INTRODUCTION

have a lot on your plate. With this in mind, there are a few things to help you out:

- I've kept the book short and to the point so you can quickly absorb the ideas without adding extra stress to your day.

- At the end of each chapter, you'll find a **Key Takeaways** section summarizing the main points and insights. If you're short on time, feel free to jump straight to these quick hits—they are designed to give you the essential points without the extra fluff. But if you want the whole experience and all the juicy details, dive into the chapter itself.

- To truly change your perspective, it's all about taking action. Check out the **Vibe Shifters** for prompts that will help you put your chapter insights into action.

- Throughout Fired Up! I have included extra resources (like videos and visuals) to help you explore the content further. Simply scan the QR code below or head to kafilondon.com/firedup and follow the **Resources** link. You'll find everything you need to spark your curiosity as you explore all the extras.

kafilondon.com/firedup

Whether you need to boost your mojo, gauge the energy of others before taking action, or want to shift the vibe of a gathering - grab *Fired Up!* whenever you need a jolt of energy.

To be clear, this book is not about the metaphysical and spiritual side of energy – I leave that to experts like Deepak Chopra, who nails it in his best-selling book, *The Seven Spiritual Laws of Success*.[2] Chopra's expertise blends spiritual wisdom with advice on how cosmic energy flows through everything. I have learned a ton from him and encourage you to reference his work for insight. Here, we're diving into a different type of energy, your personal energy, and how you can leverage it to impact others positively.

Fired Up! is for those who find themselves leading others, whether by title, position, or circumstance. Let's think of leading others as a mindset – a way of being that can be embodied by anyone in any role. True leadership comes from within and is reflected in how we interact, motivate and guide those around us in our everyday lives.

You could be a workplace mentor or someone who guides new employees and helps them navigate challenges. Perhaps you're a community member who coordinates local events, rallies volunteers, or drives projects. Maybe you're a parent who provides direction and inspiration to family members, an athlete who motivates teammates and fosters team spirit without wearing the captain's armband, or an online community moderator who manages discussions and supports new members.

This book is for natural leaders–those who inspire and influence others regardless of position or title.

Energy has a reach that extends beyond what meets the eye. It's a dance of frequencies that has the power to create connections, light up a room, and influence the decisions of those around you.

As we explore through these pages, I invite you to embrace in an energetic experiment that will help you shift your perspective.

INTRODUCTION

My hope is that *Fired Up!* helps you create energy so you can turn up turned on, and transfer that energy into positive ripples that shift and uplift how others around you feel.

Ready? Let's ride!

PART 1

WHY PERSON-TO-PEOPLE ENERGY MATTERS

CHAPTER ONE

Energy Is Everything

"We are all connected by energy, invisible threads that shape our reality and influence our relationships."

- ANONYMOUS

It'd make sense to kick off with a definition of the main event here, but energy is easier to recognize than define. You know it when you see it: a speeding motorcycle on a wide-open road, a frisbee elegantly flying through the air, the instant calm found in the company of a good friend, 30,000 voices singing together at a gig, or a group of four-year-olds running around in circles after ingesting Jelly Beans by the fistful.

Scientists[3] define it as: *"the capacity for doing work,"* but that doesn't necessarily make things any clearer because physicists use the term "work" in a way that doesn't directly translate to our day-to-day lives.

In a more everyday context, energy could be considered a property of something that moves and gives off heat, sound, or light.

Energy is all around us; it's the essence that drives the universe.

You might be familiar with some of its different forms – kinetic, thermal, electrical, chemical, nuclear, and the like.

But the energy we are talking about in this book is *people energy*. More specifically, *person-to-people energy*. It's the positive kind that radiates from one person to many people, spreading contagiously like a laugh or a yawn, creating a ripple that spreads like wildfire.

What does energetic leadership look like?

In 1992, I made the bold decision to accept an international job transfer, leave my father, siblings, nieces, and nephews behind in London, and move across the pond to work as a management consultant in the US.

In 1993, I met Tom Brown.

Tom was a tall, statuesque, accomplished white American man. He was mature, seasoned, and established, with a background in law. I, on the other hand, was young, impressionable, and eager to embrace the next chapter of my career after getting laid off from my first real corporate job since graduating.

At the time, we were both employees of a boutique management consulting firm, DA Consulting Group. We teamed up from across the country, tackling client projects together.

Tom stood out. With his commanding presence, he instantly caught my attention and left me curious. Working with him wasn't just about getting the job done; it was *how* he showed up that made all the difference.

Tom made you feel like leading others was more than just a job – it was a privilege.

The moment he walked into a room, you could feel the atmosphere change. It was like the air shifted; everyone would quiet down and listen in awe. It was pretty amazing to see. I learned so much about presence, authority, and leadership from this great master. He has greatly influenced who I am today and was, no doubt, the spark that ignited the careers of many of my peers who now hold senior executive leadership roles in global organizations.

While conducting research for this book, I often thought of Tom. What made him stand out so much?

It wasn't just his title or his way of doing things. It was something else, something you could almost see but not quite touch.

It was his energy.

He had incredible energy. We inexperienced consultants were all eyes and ears, just soaking in how he worked his magic. Tom was like an energy magnet whose presence and conviction told their own story. His leadership style effortlessly oozed wisdom, expertise, and enthusiasm. Clients loved him, and his direct reports loved him even more.

We've all been around leaders who are a walking battery of good vibes. Beyond experience, expertise, or even charisma, there is something that you feel the urge to plug into. They walk the walk and radiate energy that lights up the room and shifts the soul.

Even after he was promoted from being my peer to being my boss, Tom was never about posturing or using his position to command power. Nope, he was all about building trust and setting the right vibe in the team.

But let's be real – not every leader is like Tom. In fact, the world of leadership is often far from this ideal. For many, leading others can be a bumpy ride filled with hurdles, demands, and deadlines that can drain even the best of us. If you've been around the block a few times, you'll know exactly what I'm talking about. But how can you avoid it? How can you transform from basking in someone else's glow to being the lighthouse yourself? How can you be more like Tom?

I could see that Tom's pull was all about positive relational energy (though I didn't have the words for it at the time). Leading with positive relational energy is not just about being in charge; it's about being a force of positivity that becomes a ripple for others to connect with. When you lead with energy, you switch from being energized to being the energy source. You are not just leading, you are elevating. It's about your energy fueling the energy of others, creating a collective boost.

But we're getting ahead of ourselves. In Chapter Three, we'll explore relational energy more deeply. Before then, we have a few hurdles we need to understand before we can jump them.

Why aren't we leading with energy already?

Of course, not everyone is ready to take the reins and be the main star that lights up the sky.

In reality, great leaders are often already maxed out juggling work responsibilities. Add in the day-to-day challenges of integrating work, life, and family responsibilities, and the best leaders suffer in silence because they de-prioritize their own needs. To avoid falling into this pattern, we first need to understand the problems it involves.

ENERGY IS EVERYTHING

When you lead with energy, you switch from being energized to being the source of energy. You are not just leading, you are elevating. It's about your energy fueling the energy of others, creating a collective boost.

I've observed three pain points repeatedly impacting leaders' energy: exhaustion, uncertainty, and disengagement. Let's examine each one more closely.

Problem 1: The exhaustion trap

Those responsible for leading others are often faced with juggling what feels like a million things at once. The stress and pressure can be overwhelming, and it's not long before exhaustion sets in. This isn't just a personal issue. Burnout leaves us without enough fuel in the tank to show up, lead others energetically, and get the job done. Eventually, other team members feel the effect. The once bright and dynamic leader begins to fade, and the impact is felt across the group or organization.

Problem 2: Leading through uncertain times

Leading through uncertainty can take a real toll on our energy. When faced with unpredictable challenges, it can feel like we are running on a self-adjusting treadmill, trying to hold a steady pace while the belt speeds up and slows down under our feet, all by itself! This constant state of flux demands a lot from us mentally and emotionally. Such uncertainty can sap our energy, making it harder for us to stay motivated and engaged.

Problem 3: Leaders are disengaging

Losing self-motivation can be the beginning of a decline in personal energy and enthusiasm. If our energy is funky, that funkiness will radiate out and impact our interactions with others. Can we really expect others to stay engaged with us when we're not even exciting ourselves?

As anchors for engagement, we leaders are the guiding lights that enable others to thrive. Each of these problems is a reminder of how crucial our energy and approach are in navigating the complexities of leading others.

How your energy impacts others

Dealing with change is a constant in leadership. The real challenge is getting others on board with it. Our energy as leaders plays a huge role here. If you're not fully charged, you might inadvertently spread doubt and resistance. On the flip side, you could be the driving force that inspires the team to embrace new ideas and directions.

Picture this: a leader walks in carrying a bunch of stress, irritability, or anxiety. It's like they are walking around casting a shadow over everything. They dampen the mood like a rain cloud at a picnic.

This kind of energy can be toxic. It seeps into every corner, stifling creativity, weakening teamwork, and bringing down the whole team's spirit. It's like a silent storm that nobody really talks about but everyone feels.

To help us navigate this storm, I've created **The Energy Ladder of Impact**, a simple yet powerful tool for determining and bringing awareness to how energized (or drained) you might be. More than just a measuring stick, it's a roadmap to guide you upwards, enhancing both your personal resilience and the performance of those you affect.

The ladder has six rungs, each representing a different energy level from drained to energized: fed up, frustrated, fine, focused, flourishing, and fired up! Each level of the ladder can also be identified by a state of mind – this is designed to give you a better awareness of how you are showing up. The third column shows the level of positive impact; it reflects how you influence others.

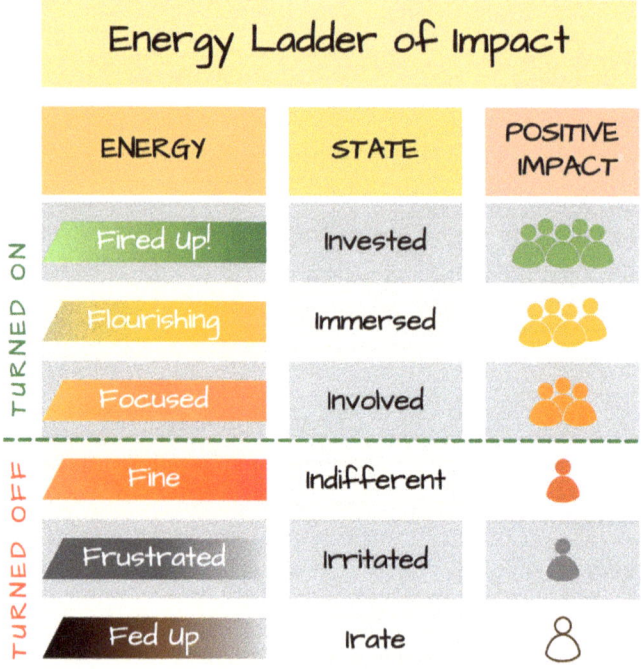

Where do you land on the ladder, and where do you want to go? Let's take a closer look at each rung so you can place yourself accurately.

Fed up and frustrated

From the lower tiers of the ladder, our fed up and frustrated energy likely translates negatively to others. This is where we bring down people in our circles of influence. Stress, negativity, and all that not-so-great stuff hang out.

Most of us can end up stuck here for longer than necessary when we are consumed with something annoying that has already happened, or with the anxiety of the possibility of something happening in the future. This leaves us feeling irritated or even downright irate, and that funky energy seeps out to others.

When you're fed up or frustrated, the air around you gets heavier. Before you know it, there's a sign slapped on your forehead that reads: CAUTION, *Vibe Killer*.

I sometimes notice myself feeling drained after spending time with certain people. I sense a heaviness in their energy that impacts me deeply. It's like they are pulling me into their web of negativity. My instinct is to distance myself from them as quickly as possible to preserve my own wellbeing. This instinct isn't exactly compassionate – and it's also a little hypocritical. We all have moments when our energy is not at its best, and we unintentionally bring a negative vibe to those around us. I am no exception; my funks burden others too, so I'm putting in the work to become more mindful of the energy I take in and the energy I put out.

If you're stuck in the low rungs, you are not being your best or doing your best work. You are leaking energy. Perhaps you are feeling disconnected from your role or purpose or dealing with frustrations, irritations, or even deeper feelings that are demotivating.

What differentiates the best from the rest is the ability to recognize these circumstances and seek change.

Acknowledging that our energy can stay negative in these lower tiers means we can also take responsibility for shifting it upwards and uplifting those around us.

Fine

As we ascend the ladder, our personal energy shifts from negative to positive. Midway through the climb, we reach a neutral point – *Fine*.

When your energy is fine, you're not dragging people down… but you're not exactly lifting them up either.

Initially, *Fine* can seem like a stable, easy place to be. But settling here can have a significant negative impact on you and others. From this stable, easy, 'fine' place, predictability threatens your energy and opens it up to stagnation. When routine activities require less mental and emotional effort, you may start disengaging. Over time, this results in a lack of enthusiasm, which causes energy levels to plateau and decay.

Ironically, a lack of stimulating challenges can lead to burnout characterized by boredom and dissatisfaction. A monotonous routine can drain emotional energy and ultimately affect well-being and interpersonal relationships.

In the coming chapters, we will unpack the process of taking meaningful, proactive steps to build resilience and sustain enthusiasm, leading to a more vibrant and dynamic presence that will shift you upwards away from fine.

Focused

Shifting from the tedious neutrality of *Fine* to the positive promise of *Focused* is a sign you are engaged, in the zone, and actively contributing to whatever the game is you have in-play.

When your energy is focused, you're in a powerful position to stretch your potential and reach even greater heights. Your positive energy is resonating with others, whether you are intentional about it or not.

Flourishing and Fired Up!

The top rungs, *Flourishing* and *Fired Up!* are where the real magic happens.

This is where positive relational energy lives (more on this later). We're talking about enthusiasm, motivation, and all that good juicy stuff that gets people energized. This is where you inspire, drive change, and create an environment where everyone feels like they can conquer the world.

This is where you lead with energy.

If I were a betting woman, I'd guess you're here because you want to kick ass and take action, so let's get real about where you stand on The Energy Ladder of Impact – are you fed up or fired up?

To help you out, I've created a tool to help you figure out if you are leading with the energy you need to be your most awesome self. Think of it as a quick check up or a simple audit. By taking the audit, you'll get a sense of whether your mojo is thriving or slowly leaking like air from a flat tire.

Side note: If you are ready to dive in and discover whether you're rocking your leadership with the energy of a dynamo or if it's time to recharge your batteries, head over to: kafilondon.com/energyaudit.

Okay, I digressed, so let's get back to the point. Think of this ladder as a guide to gauging how your personal energy levels can impact the people around you. It's not just about being an annoying cheerleader who is perpetually *on*; it's about being aware of where your energy is and how it's positively or negatively influencing others.

As we explore the next section, keep The Energy Ladder of Impact in mind. It'll help us see how shifting our energy can make a huge difference in tackling exhaustion, uncertainty and disengagement.

ENERGY IS EVERYTHING

Key Takeaways

1. Energy is everything and is everywhere. It exists in different forms, for example, kinetic, thermal, electrical, chemical, and nuclear. The energy we are focusing on is *relational energy*.

2. It's the positive kind that radiates from one person to many people, spreading contagiously like a laugh or a yawn, creating a ripple that spreads like wildfire. We're calling it *person-to-people energy*.

3. Great leaders tap into positive relational energy as their secret weapon. It's not just about being in charge; it's about being a force of positivity that becomes a ripple for others to connect with.

4. Leading with energy helps you tap into your own power and use it as a source to illuminate others.

5. With the never-ending work-life struggle, most leaders experience the same three energy-draining points repeatedly: exhaustion, uncertainty, and disengagement.

6. The Energy Ladder of Impact is a tool that correlates our level of energy (Fed up, Frustrated, Fine, Focused, Flourishing or Fired Up!) to the amount of impact (negative to positive) we have on others.

If you are curious and would like to discover where you fall on the Energy Ladder of Impact, head to kafilondon.com/energyaudit or scan the QR Code to take the audit.

kafilondon.com/energyaudit

Vibe Shifters

Use the following prompts to help put your chapter insights into action.

1. What message is your energy sending to others – does it inspire action or cause eye rolls?
2. How do you show up at work when the pressure is on? Do you rally the troops or spread the stress?
3. How would others describe the energy you bring to the table?
4. List five words that describe how you might feel (physically and emotionally) when you are fed up or frustrated.
5. What does being "fine" mean for you – and what does hanging out there cost you?
6. What words describe your feelings when you are flourishing or fired up?
7. What role do you play in team dynamics – are you a connector or disconnector?
8. What story are you telling yourself about your energy – are you owning it or letting it own you?
9. Who are the people whose energy you admire most and what makes their vibe so magnetic?
10. What does leading with energy look like to you and what could you achieve by doing more of it?

CHAPTER TWO

The Transfer of Energy

"Energy, like currency, can be spent, saved or invested. How you choose to use it determines the wealth of your future."

— ELLEN ROGIN[4]

The perpetuity of energy is magical. We can wave our wands and share it with others in a heartbeat (deliberately or accidentally!). In this chapter, we're going to explore the moments in which energy is transferred so that we can move to do so more deliberately.

Energy as currency

Currency is typically associated with money. It serves as a medium of exchange between buyers and sellers, providing a measure of value for goods and services. However, the concept of currency can be extended beyond its economic role to other valuable commodities, such as human energy.

Just like money, the energy we bring into our interactions and daily activities has value and can impact our personal and professional lives, so paying attention to how we generate and manage it is key. Just as a bank account is a container for holding money, our body is a container for holding energy. Let's take a second to compare the two at a high level.

- **Generating it:** Generally, generating income requires an investment of time, effort, skills and resources (like working a job, running a business, or making investments). Likewise, sourcing and generating energy requires an investment in our mental, physical, and emotional well-being.

- **Managing it**: Economic currency can inflate and deflate, and so can our energy levels. Like money, energy can be stored and drawn upon when needed. Building a bank of emotional resilience can yield significant returns so it is accessible when needed.

- **Spending it**: Just as economic currency facilitates financial trade and transfers, energy facilitates exchanges in professional and social situations (for example, how we influence, motivate and inspire those around us).

In *First Things First*, Stephen R. Covey, A. Roger Merrill, and Rebecca R. Merrill brought currencies to life, referring to the various forms of value we exchange with others to improve our relationships and interactions: time, attention, recognition, and support.[5]

Exchanging currencies is about recognizing and respecting what others value. Think of energy as an extension of these currencies. Just like time and recognition, when you bring energy to your interactions it's a game-changer - it can uplift the mood, create a stronger connection, and inspire others to engage more fully. When you bring positive energy into a conversation, it doesn't just help you connect better with others; it sets the tone, builds

THE TRANSFER OF ENERGY

When you bring positive energy into a conversation, it doesn't just help you connect better with others; it sets the tone, builds trust, and can even turn an ordinary interaction into something memorable and powerful.

trust, and can even turn an ordinary interaction into something memorable and powerful.

Understanding and leveraging these currencies can create win-win situations in personal and professional relationships and achieve better outcomes.

From sunshine to synergy

The energy journey starts with sunshine. Plants capture the sun's energy through photosynthesis. We then eat plants (or products from the animals that eat them) to get that stored energy.

Scientists Paul D. Boyer and John E. Walker won the Nobel Prize in 1997 for their discoveries around how our bodies convert food into a currency of energy called adenosine triphosphate (ATP).[6] ATP is like a rechargeable battery that powers all the work our cells do.

When we move, work, and create, we convert our ATP into other energetic currencies to charge others' batteries. In practice, this might look like teaching, creating, or speaking. Our energy can be converted in this way to create value for people, who can then pass it on further. Kicked off by sunshine, it's a continuous cycle of energy transformation that allows us to impact others.

Next, we'll unlock the doors to impact as we explore how leading with energy is your passport to making waves in the world.

Key Takeaways

1. By thinking of our energy as a form of currency, we can better appreciate its value and manage it more effectively.

2. Different sources of income set the base for financial stability and wealth-building strategies. In the same way, your behaviors, habits, and activities provide the fuel for the resilience of your mind and body.

3. Just as you would carefully manage your finances, it's super important to be mindful of how you manage your energy. Whether you manage your own investments or outsource the responsibilities to a trusted financial professional, it's important to prioritize how you manage your energetic assets.

4. Sharing monetary wealth allows us to improve the welfare of others; sharing positive energy can inspire and lift others.

Vibe Shifters

Use the following prompts to help put your chapter insights into action.

1. How often do you check your energy levels compared to your bank balance and what does that say about where you focus your attention?

2. If your energy were a stock, would it be booming or tanking? How can you boost its value and improve your return on investment?

3. How are you managing your energy? Like your finances, are you using it wisely, or letting it slip away on things that drain you?

4. How would your life skyrocket if you managed your energy with the same focus and drive you apply to your finances?

5. How can investing wisely in other people's energy supercharge your own success and take your game to the next level?

For additional resources related to energy as currency, head to kafilondon.com/firedup or scan the QR Code below and follow the **Resources** link.

kafilondon.com/firedup

CHAPTER THREE

The Ripple Effect

"Just as ripples spread out when a single pebble is dropped into the water, the action of individuals can have a far-reaching effect."

- DALAI LAMA[7]

It was a sunny afternoon at Clissold Park in North London. The scent of freshly cut grass filled the air, and a gentle breeze carried the laughter of children playing. My brother, Abi, and I were young teens enjoying the freedom and openness the park offered up.

With arms spread out wide like wings, we zigged and zagged our way to the lake. It was time to practice our throwing skills by playing Ducks and Drakes, a game in which you throw stones across the water, trying to make them bounce and skip along the surface before they inevitably sink.

That day, we spent what felt like an hour gathering the smoothest, flattest stones – ones that felt just right in the palm. When I'd collected as many stones as I could hold in my small hand, I joined Abi at the edge of the lake to watch

> the magic happen. He was the real pro; I was there to watch in awe.
>
> With a flick of his wrist, he sent the first stone dancing over the water, creating ripples for each bounce.
>
> I watched, eyes wide, as the ripples spread out in perfect circles, eventually disappearing into the lake's vastness.

It's crazy to imagine that this simple act would stay with me throughout my life and become a powerful metaphor for the work I love doing today.

Understanding the ripple effect

I now understand that the ripples I saw spread across the pond are a visual representation of relational energy (which we'll explore in detail in the next few pages). Think about the pebbles we cast into the pond of life. The energy behind each pebble creates ripples that shape lives, teams, communities, and organizations.

Mine and Abi's presence at the lake that day reminds us that energy is not just about us. Our actions, words, and being create ripples extending far beyond us.

Rippling examples

Over the years, I have attended my fair share of workshops and conferences. One of the most memorable workshops I attended was on the Filofax system.

In case you are not familiar with the original Filofax, it's basically a manual paper-based planning system that involves using a leather-bound personal planner. The Filofax system has tons of inserts that were supposed to be logical, functional and easy to use. The truth is, the whole system confused the hell out of me... so I signed myself up for a workshop by the creators of the system – Franklin Covey!

On the day of the event, the facilitator burst into the room like a ray of sunshine, completely brimming with confidence and positivity. It was infectious. He was such a pro that whatever he wanted us to do, we all tapped into his energy and responded enthusiastically. Since it was a public workshop, most of us had never met before. However, we collaborated openly and gave it our all.

I attended that workshop more than twenty years ago, but that facilitator's ripples are still bouncing around, so much so that I am writing in this book, and you, yes, you, are feeling his impact! Now that is one heck of a positive ripple the Covey trainer put out into the world!

In a different scenario, a coaching client shared how she felt about her new team leader, Jack, when she accepted a new position at a prestigious national bank.

Jack was about six feet tall, had a slight frame and walked around all day with his head down and eyes peeping just above the rim of his wire glasses.

He dragged himself around the office like the weight of the world was on his shoulders. His energy was heavy, and his mood uncertain at best; people never knew what to expect.

Team members picked up on his vibe and found themselves being cautious and hesitant around him. Their work had no real passion; it was more a means to an end. Each day felt like a grind, only to be rewarded with a silent nod or a muffled grunt when Jack acknowledged the successful completion of assigned tasks. Jack's heavy energy hung around like a bad smell, seeping into every corner of the office. Soon enough, the team started associating the heavy vibe with their jobs, and it was not long before they were craving a place with better energy to work in.

This is a perfect example of how negative energy in action can spread and impact everyone around them.

Your energy, whether a radiant beam of positivity or a cloud of negativity, is a pebble that sets waves in motion.

And, the ripple effect doesn't stop with those in your direct circle of influence; it travels through the corridors of your group, community or organization, shaping its culture, innovation, and performance.

Just as a single stone creates ripples in the water, your energy sets off waves that begin with you. When you embrace your role as a leading source of positive energy, you become the pebble that sets change in motion and has the power to influence the landscape around you.

It's not just about how you feel; it's about how you make others feel. It's about the vibe you bring into the room, the enthusiasm you infuse into your team, and the impact you have on their performance and well-being.

Your energy isn't confined to the walls of your surroundings; it permeates every interaction, every decision, and every moment of your day. It's a dynamic dance that not only transforms how you show up, but how you can be the catalyst to ignite change with those you come into contact with.

THE RIPPLE EFFECT

By leading with energy, you not only set the tone for those around you, but also inspire them to do the same.

When you embrace your pebble power, you'll notice something incredible: the ripple you create will become a wave of transformation. By leading with energy, you not only set the tone for those around you, but also inspire them to do the same.

This is an invitation to embark on a journey that will amplify your visibility, enrich your impact, and leave an indelible mark on everything and everyone your energy touches.

Amani's superpowers

When your energy evokes positive responses, it's like a fascinating dance. Your energy sets the rhythm, and others join in. Seeing my five-year-old great-niece boogieing at a birthday party is a joyful example of this.

> *Like her mum, Amani loves to dance. I watch as she bops her little head happily; she's the only one on the dance floor. Within a few minutes, a handful of brave kids have joined her. Then some shyer kids, too. By the end of the song, all the kids at the party have caught the vibe and are happily grooving along, leaning into their own moves.*
>
> *All Amani cared about was moving her body and having a great time. By doing so, she made it okay to dance, and the simple act of sharing her energy invited others to do the same.*

Through dancing, Amani demonstrates two superpowers: relational energy and flowing authenticity. These powers are available to everyone if we choose to tap into them. Let's take a closer look at both.

Relational energy

Just as Amani had the power to pull everyone into her orbit as she lit up the dance floor, imagine if that kind of pure, unfiltered joy and enthusiasm could be harnessed in your workplace.

That's exactly what Baker, Cross, and Parker explored in their 2003 article, "*What Creates Energy in Organizations.*"[8] They discovered the energy people bring into the workplace can have a profound impact. The "energizers" light up the space around them. They are the ones who make ideas flow freely, sparking enthusiasm and increasing productivity. When people around us are buzzing with positive vibes, it actually boosts how well we feel, work, and learn.

But not everyone brings that type of positive energy. Baker, Cross, and Parker also talked about the "de-energizers"—those folks who, instead of lighting up the room, seem to dim the light, dragging everyone down and making work feel like a slog instead of a dance party.

Sounds great, right? But the real magic behind it was unclear.

In 2015, Owens et al. conducted a series of studies showing there was something to this person-to-people energy thing in business, and they coined the term "relational energy", which is defined as:

> "...the positive feeling and increased resourcefulness experienced as a direct result of interaction with someone else."[9]

We spoke a little about relational energy in chapter one, and I promised we'd explore it more later... well, here we are!

Harvard researchers have found that what sets outstanding leaders apart isn't charisma, influence, power, knowledge, experience, or even expertise. The one thing that scores more points than all these factors is positive relational energy.[10]

Similarly, a 2023 Forbes article states relational energy impacts employee engagement. The article goes on to reference a Gallup survey that reports teams with higher engagement see more productivity, lower turnover and better customer loyalty.[11]

Relational energy and its super-spreader sidekick, emotional contagion, shape the energetic vibe of every interaction and group.

Emotional contagion is how relational energy spreads. Through facial expressions, tone of voice, movement, and body language, one person's energy and mood can set the tone for the whole group. We saw this in Amani – her happy dancing energy triggered a chain reaction. One person's authenticity can start a dance party like a spark can ignite a wildfire.

When you're in a good mood and show it, people around you pick up on those vibes and start feeling good, too; they catch your mood. Likewise, it's hard for those around you not to catch your misery if you're feeling miserable. Emotions can touch and change others quickly and directly.

But the effect of your relational energy is long-lasting. It's like a lamp – when it is on (or positive), it casts a warm, inviting glow over everyone in the room, creating a cozy, energizing atmosphere. The lamp's light consistently fills the entire space, even as its surroundings change. When we radiate positive relational energy, the resulting impact can ripple through a group, boosting morale, engagement, effective collaboration, motivation, well-being, and productivity. People become more engaged, committed, and enthusiastic.

Do you think those benefits are confined to the room you're in? Of course not! The surroundings become a thriving ecosystem, and feeling good together opens the door for magic to happen elsewhere, too.

On the flip side, when your relational energy triggers negative responses, the consequences can be detrimental. Leading with negative relational energy is like leading with the lamp off. In the darkness, it's hard to stay engaged, communicate well, or be productive. People may disengage and become disinterested or demotivated. Communication breakdowns occur, leading to misunderstandings and conflicts. Productivity suffers, and morale takes a nosedive.

There's an art to getting the balance right – when to be invigorating, when to be calming, when to be empowering, when to step back and be supportive. Just like an indoor spin class, it's about creating an atmosphere that is both motivating and supportive, where energy flows freely but does not overwhelm. Finding this balance takes skill and intuition.

Relational energy by default can be negative or neutral, but the possibilities are endless when we grab it by the horns and make it our fuel of choice. By actively using our relational energy, we are leveraging emotional contagion to create ripples of epic impact with every interaction.

Flowing into relational energy through authenticity

In today's fast-moving world, we tend to focus on visible achievements, skills, and accolades. But what about the potent yet often overlooked force that shapes the course of our lives? The force that doesn't show up in resumes but can change the course of your day, your interactions, and even your destiny!

We are talking about energy, a dynamic and intangible essence that radiates from within us and impacts everyone we come into contact with.

Because we're so accustomed to measuring success by external metrics like ticking boxes and collecting achievements, we often forget the most essential part of our human experience: how we feel and how we make others feel through our energy.

This feeling is our greatest asset. It's the silent conductor of the symphony of life that guides our actions, decisions, and how we connect with others.

While we can't see energy, we can absolutely feel it. Think about walking into a room and finding that person, the Tom Brown whose energy lights up the atmosphere. Maybe it's the colleague who always radiates positivity, or that friend who makes you feel instantly at ease. That's the magic of energy. You can't always put your finger on it but, boy, can you feel it.

Your energy isn't totally intangible, though; it's your signature. It carries the wisdom of your expertise, the flavor of your essence, and the uniqueness of your expressions. It's the fingerprint of who you are. It's a blend of your values, identity, beliefs, and expressions.

So, finding your energy requires knowing yourself. If you can be entirely yourself, like Amani, you'll no doubt find your own contagious energy and be the catalyst for others finding their own. Tapping into your most impactful energy requires blatant authenticity.

But... where can we find our authenticity?

Have you ever been so absorbed with something that you lose track of time? Maybe a work project, a hobby or even a fabulous conversation? That is what Mihaly Csikszentmihalyi calls *Flow*.[12] It's that juicy spot where you are fully immersed in your zone of awesomeness and not even thinking about the activity you're carrying out.

Now, how do you feel during these moments of flow? Amazing, energized, and focused, right? You are tapped into your authentic self – into your energy.

And the energy doesn't just stay with you; it ripples and radiates out to affect those around you, too!

Imagine you are in a meeting and in that flow state; your energy, enthusiasm, and level of engagement are contagious. Your team picks up your positive vibe and it boosts their mood and productivity, too.

Csikszentmihalyi's work on flow demonstrates how interconnected we all are and how our energy can create waves of positive change that inspire greatness and leave an everlasting mark on others.

How ripples turn into waves

When we talk about positive relational energy, we're talking about interactions that uplift, inspire, and connect us. Each positive interaction creates a ripple, spreading outward and influencing others. Your energy doesn't just stop with you; it moves through your network, impacting everyone you interact with, turning into a tidal wave of positivity.

But how exactly does that happen? Let's examine the moving parts.

- **Shared purpose**
    - **Unified goals**: When people come together with a common goal, like a team working towards a project deadline or a group pushing through a challenging workout, it amplifies relational energy. This shared purpose creates powerful bonds and a unified drive.
    - **Emotional connection**: Experiencing the same highs and lows together strengthens emotional bonds. Whether it's celebrating a win or supporting each other through challenges, these shared moments build deeper connections.
- **Increased engagement**
    - **Active involvement**: Just like you give your all in a group activity, when everyone is actively involved, the energy soars. Everyone contributes and feels like an essential part of the group.
    - **Contagious enthusiasm**: High energy levels are infectious. One person's enthusiasm can lift the whole group, creating a dynamic and engaging atmosphere.

- **Mutual empowerment**
    - **Supportive environment**: When emotional contagion carries positive relational energy, people feel valued and supported. It's like having a cheer squad boosting your confidence and encouraging you to push harder.
    - **Collaborative spirit**: Shared energy promotes collaboration. People are more willing to help each other, share ideas, and work together towards common goals if there is a sense of community.

- **Creativity and innovation**
    - **Synergy of ideas**: The buzz of collective energy often sparks creativity and innovation. When everyone's energized and connected, they're more likely to come up with brilliant ideas and solutions.
    - **Safe space for exploration**: A high-energy, supportive environment encourages risk-taking and exploration, leading to exciting breakthroughs.

- **Resilience and strength**
    - **Shared resilience**: Facing challenges together builds resilience. The collective energy and support help everyone bounce back stronger from setbacks.
    - **Strength in numbers**: There's power in unity. When you feel part of a cohesive group, you're more likely to stand firm and overcome obstacles together.

Key Takeaways

1. The simple joy of tossing pebbles into a pond and watching the ripples expand is a great metaphor for the impact of your energy's ability to spread far and wide.

2. Your energy, whether positive or negative, is contagious. It is a catalyst for change and sets the tone for those around you, affecting morale and performance.

3. The energy ripple starts with you, but it is not limited in its reach; you may be an energy source, but your energy extends beyond you and radiates to your community's culture and overall success.

4. My great-niece's dance moves (and psychologist Mihaly Csikszentmihalyi's research) show us that by cultivating our own flow from authenticity, the positive energy we generate inspires and uplifts others.

5. What sets outstanding leaders apart isn't charisma, influence, power, knowledge, experience, or even expertise. The one thing that scores more points than all these factors is positive relational energy.

Vibe Shifters

Use the following prompts to help put your chapter insights into action.

1. How are you showing up for others – are you bringing the energy that lights people up or are you dimming the room?
2. When you connect with someone, do they walk away feeling charged and ready to conquer or drained and defeated?
3. What ripple effect are you creating with your energy - are you creating waves or just treading water?
4. What kind of legacy is your energy leaving behind? Are people better off because of your vibe, or is there room for a bigger impact?
5. How intentional are you about setting the vibe versus just going with the flow?

For additional resources related to the ripple effect, head to kafilondon.com/firedup or scan the QR Code below and follow the **Resources** link.

kafilondon.com/firedup

PART 2

HOW TO LEAD WITH ENERGY

CHAPTER FOUR

The Fired Up! Framework

"Each of us has the power to light a fire and be the ignition for others."

- JIM ZIOLKOWSKI[13]

With the groundwork laid in Part 1, we are ready to kick things into high gear and dive into how to lead with energy.

Whether you are leading a team, running your own show or just trying to elevate your daily interactions, a toxic vibe can feel like you are stuck in the dark – and because we know negativity spreads like wildfire, it drags everyone (including you) down. When we connect with others, we can unintentionally dump our own heaviness on them, leaving them feeling drained, unmotivated, or even freaked out. These lose-lose situations create a cloud of negativity that messes with communication, connection, and impact.

But here's the deal, just like plants turn towards the sun for growth and nourishment, people naturally gravitate towards positive energy. That's the heliotropic effect in action.

By tapping into a simple three-part framework, you can become the light others are magnetically drawn to. They might not even know why, but they'll keep coming back for more because your energy is exactly what they need to thrive.

Enter *The Fired Up! Framework*.

This framework will guide you through attuning your energy, exploring and assessing the energy of others, and then shifting the group's energy (yours and theirs) to where you want it to be.

Here's how it breaks down, *Tune Up*, *Sync Up*, and *Lift Up*.

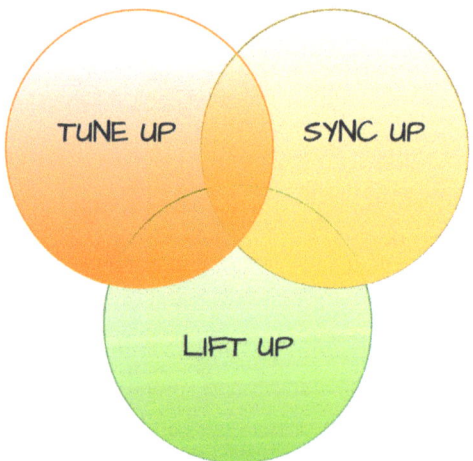

- **Tune Up**: When you top up your tank and optimize your energy, you're running at full capacity – fully charged and ready to crush it – that is when you are "in the zone"
- **Sync Up**: If you want your message to land with others, you have to know where they are starting from. Understanding

people's current energetic state gives you the insight to meet them where they are, build trust and guide them in a way that actually clicks.

- **Lift Up:** When you set the tone and lead the charge with your energy, you create a contagious vibe that elevates everyone around you. Suddenly, inspiring and uplifting others is a breeze. Your vibrant enthusiasm sparks a chain reaction encouraging others to step up their game.

In the following chapters, we're going to focus on each of the three circles that make up the Venn diagram of The Fired Up! Framework.

Ready to tune up your own energy, sync with others', and lift your group's vibe?

Great. Let's go!

CHAPTER FIVE

Tune Up

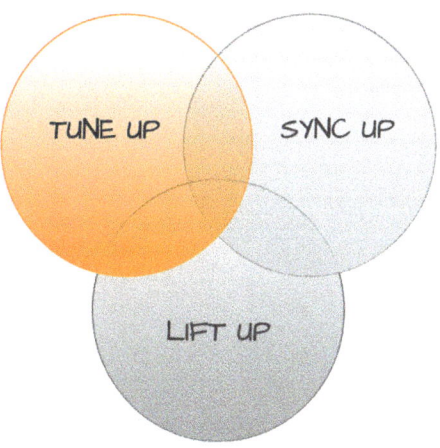

Tuning up is all about optimizing your energy. If you've lost your mojo or your work has you feeling overwhelmed and overworked, this chapter will help you reconnect to who you really are, reignite your fire, and get your light shining again. Trust me, I have been through this phase a few times myself – when work kicked my butt and had me feeling stressed and a hot mess – it was a flashing sign to recalibrate and take back control.

Tuning up your energy starts with recognizing and owning your Sparkability Factor.

Sparkability Factor

Your ability to positively impact others is your Sparkability Factor.

Think of it as your 'X' factor or the power that drives your mojo. To simplify things further, it's based on the following key igniters.

- **Your vitality**: the capacity to stay vibrant and full of energy
- **Your vibe**: who you are and what you stand for
- **Your value:** how you share your experience and expertise
- **Your voice:** what you say and how you say it
- **Your visibility**: how you show up and express yourself.

By tuning up these five igniters, you'll not only align with your own energy but also spark the fire in others.

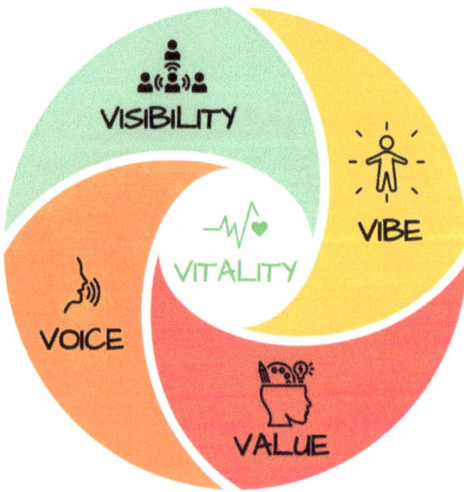

Your Sparkability Factor focuses on the inner work necessary to rewire your fire and stay vibrant. Notice how vitality sits in the

TUNE UP

Your ability to positively impact others is your Sparkability Factor.

Think of it as your 'X' factor or the power that drives your mojo. It is based on five key igniters: your vitality, your vibe, your value, your voice and your visibility.

middle? That's because without vitality, our vibe, value, voice, and visibility wane.

With that in mind, we'll start with the self-work that will build your vitality and set you up for success. This will provide a solid foundation from which your Sparkability can thrive. Once we've got that down, we'll circle-back to talk more about the other four igniters: your vibe, value, voice and visibility.

Vitality

Before we can dive into how to light others up, we need to focus on you. If you run on empty, your ability to ignite others is seriously limited. That's why finding your vitality (the lifeblood of energetic leadership) through self-care is the first step in tuning up and aligning with your energy. Inner work is vital to leading with energy and creating impact. The real magic is having the energetic capacity to serve people in a way that encourages them to shift.

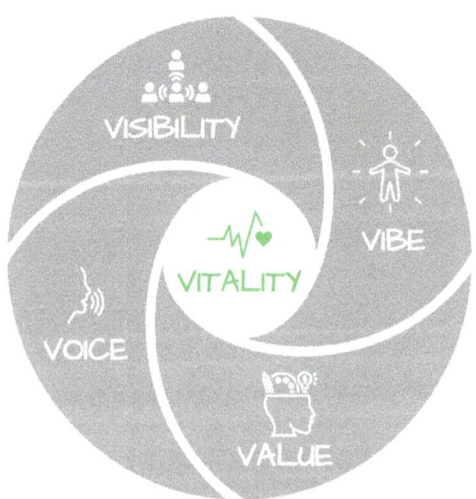

Our energy can be off or low because life gets in the way. Stress, exhaustion, and day-to-day chaos can drain us. Without recharging mentally, physically, and emotionally, it's tough to bring our best selves to the table and positively pour into others.

The signs of a steady downhill are clear: We run out of juice, lose our mojo, become totally apathetic, and start shrinking back and disengaging from life. Let's take the time to focus on our vitality. By doing so, we'll elevate our energy game before it turns into a code-red situation.

In the hustle and bustle of life, it's easy to get caught up in the fast lane, racing from one commitment to the next. But here's the truth (that we know but for some reason choose to ignore): we can't run on empty.

Imagine your energy as the fuel that powers your journey. Just as a car can't go far without gasoline, it becomes more challenging to lead others effectively when your energy tank is running low.

If energy is the lifeblood of our ability to do work that results in impact, then running around with an empty tank (or one on the verge of being empty) takes a toll on our well-being, relationships, and effectiveness as a leader.

Vitality is about mindset, mood, and motivation; each is crucial for maintaining high energy levels and strong leadership skills.

- **Mindset**: Your mindset is the engine that powers your creativity, decision-making, and problem-solving mojo. When you are rocking a growth mindset, as Carol Dweck lays out in *Mindset: The New Psychology of Success*, you are not just getting by but thriving.[14] You see challenges as growth opportunities, and you can confidently tackle them. But when your mind runs on fumes, everything else feels like an uphill battle. Mental fatigue shows up as scattered thoughts, sluggish decisions and endless cycles of procrastination.

- **Mood**: Your emotional health is the heart of your interactions and relationships. When your emotional tank is empty, it messes with your mood, patience and ability to connect with others. Emotional exhaustion leaves you irritable, moody, and feeling totally disconnected. If you find yourself snapping at people or feeling emotionally numb, it's a big red flag that your emotional energy is tapped out.

- **Motivation**: Your physical health is the foundation for everything you do. Without a strong, energized body, it's tough to keep up with the demands of work, life and leading others. Physical fatigue shows up as chronic tiredness, frequent colds, and a lack of stamina. When you're physically drained, even the simplest tasks affect your drive, and staying motivated becomes an uphill battle.

When you tap into your mindset, mood, and motivation, you boost your capacity for resilience and create a powerful shield against burnout. It is about maintaining your energy, staying strong under pressure, and showing up as the unstoppable leader you're meant to be.

Know the warning signs

It's a myth that all great leaders have triple-A-type personalities with good health. While a few fit that profile, the rest of us are not so lucky.

Top-producing leaders who inspire others are able to identify what drains their energy. They have the awareness and grit to replenish it when it is low.

In this high-octane, overstimulated, always-on lifestyle, spotting the subtle signs that your energy tank is running low is often challenging. You might be sprinting through your to-do list and day-to-day life, but are you truly fueled for the long-run? Personal accountability is key when it comes to managing your vitality. People who thrive face the problem head-on, admit what is really going on, and take action. Let's unravel the tell-tale signs that you might be running on empty.

Stress is a big one! Sure, everyone has stressful moments, like being stuck in traffic or dealing with a tough work day, but stress can become a constant issue for some people. Chronic stress is no joke; persistent symptoms can become debilitating and put you at significant risk of a range of health challenges. According to the American Psychological Association, chronic stress is linked to six major causes of death (heart disease, cancer, lung ailments, liver cirrhosis, and suicide), and more than 75% of all physician visits are for stress-related ailments.[15]

The good news? You can reduce stress in various ways, from exercising to changing your routine. The first step to reducing stress is recognizing the symptoms. Once you've identified the problem, you can start managing your stress and refueling your tank.

Recognize the signs, take action, and stay on top of your game.

With that in mind, it's time to get to know some red flags. Let's take a closer look at six of the top indicators of stress.

1. **Your memory is getting worse.** As your schedule becomes more overwhelming and your to-do list grows, it's easy to

put errors down to bog-standard forgetfulness. We're only human, right? But if your mind feels foggy and scatterbrained, it's like trying to navigate through a thick forest without a compass. This is a classic symptom of energy depletion, and stress could be the culprit.

When you crank up the pressure on your brain, you're giving it a ton of extra work. This means you end up frazzled and burn out faster.

2. **Your diet and digestion are off.** Let's be real, when you are stressed, it is all too easy to reach for comfort foods. This is a natural response to stress – stress hormones in our body tell us we need more salty, sugary, fatty foods that will give us more energy to fight whatever lion we're being attacked by. But these less nutritious food choices wreak havoc on our digestion. They might feel good in the moment, but they do not give your body the fuel it needs to function well. When your body is out of whack, it can actually increase your stress levels, and indigestion follows suit.

3. **You're not drinking enough water.** If you're constantly running on low and feeling parched, your body is sending up a distress signal. When stress is part of the picture, dehydration can sneak up on you. Stress causes your body to pump out extra hormones from your adrenal glands. These glands are also in charge of regulating fluid levels and electrolytes. When they are overworked, they can trick your body into thinking it doesn't need much water even though it really does.

4. **Your sleep is messed up!** If you find yourself in a constant cycle of daytime fatigue and restless nights, stress might be the reason you feel constantly drained and exhausted. You

may experience relentless fatigue and find yourself hitting that afternoon slump day after day, while at night, stress keeps your mind racing with worries, making it impossible to relax. Everyone is different; some find themselves having bizarre dreams or feel the urge to sleep more than usual.

5. **You get frequent colds and unexplained aches.** Your body might raise the alarm through a snotty nose and achy muscles. It's telling you the check engine light is on, so slow down before you break down! Stress often leads to involuntary muscle tension, resulting in soreness and general discomfort. But it does not stop there. When your body is constantly in fight-or-flight mode, it produces excess cortisol, which weakens the immune system. This makes you more susceptible to frequent colds and illnesses, as your body is too stressed out to fend off sickness effectively.

6. **You've lost your mojo.** You used to jump out of bed, excited about the day ahead. Now, your enthusiasm has turned into a sense of duty, and you find yourself simply going through the motions. The fire that once fueled your passion is now just a flicker. You used to thrive on challenges and new opportunities; now everything feels like a chore. Losing your passion and excitement is a clear indicator that stress is taking a toll on your well-being.

On top of that, you have noticed your patience is wearing thin, and you're snapping at people or feeling irritable for no apparent reason. Dwindling energy reserves can leave the best of us feeling irritable and stressed, which is only made harder when you factor in having to navigate fluctuating mood swings.

When a warning light pops up on our car's dashboard – *low fuel*, *check engine*, *ice warning* – we slow down or stop to address the problem. This protects us, our vehicle, and those around us. But when our personal energy tanks run on empty; we often ignore the warning signs and just power through. We know better, but struggle with doing better, and moves like this are just not sustainable.

Recognizing warning signs of stress is the first bold step in mastering the art of energy management.

The hidden costs of low energy

On a personal level, the hidden costs of low energy are significant. Your relationships take a hit as your patience wears thin and irritability ramps up. You might find yourself snapping at others or withdrawing from social interactions because you don't have the energy to engage. The isolation can lead to feelings of loneliness and skyrocket your stress levels, creating a downward spiral that is tough to break.

However, running on empty isn't just a personal struggle. The impact of low energy extends far beyond feeling tired and worn out – it permeates every aspect of your personal and professional life, like an unwelcome guest at a party.

When your energy reserves are depleted, your leadership style takes a hit. Your decision-making skills suffer, and you are more likely to make mistakes, overlook important details, and lose the clear, focused vision your circle of influence relies on. People look at you as a leader for inspiration. It's tough to provide that spark if you are running on fumes.

Others will eventually sense your lack of enthusiasm, leading to disengagement, lower morale, and decreased productivity. It is a

TUNE UP

In a world that often celebrates busyness as a badge of honor, it's easy to fall into the trap of thinking that more is better.

---

vicious cycle: the more you struggle, the more those who tap into your energy struggle, further amplifying the negative impact.

By recognizing these hidden costs, you can start tackling the root causes and take proactive steps to recharge and revitalize your energy and Sparkability Factor, making sure both your personal and professional lives flourish.

Finding balance

Finding balance while juggling the responsibilities of leading yourself and others can feel like chasing a mythical creature. Yet, it's not a myth, it's an art - a delicate dance that requires practice and patience. Let's dive in the art of balance and how it can transform the way you lead.

In a world that often celebrates busyness as a badge of honor, it's easy to fall into the trap of thinking that more is better. One afternoon, I sat down with Sarah, a dynamic leader in the high-stakes world of management consulting. Over coffee, with a voice of wisdom and weariness, she shared her story.

> *"Back then, I thought success was all about doing more," Sarah began while sipping her latte.*
>
> *"I was the queen of the hustle – late nights, endless meetings, always pushing and doing more than most thought was possible. My calendar was a nightmare, my inbox a beast, but I loved it. At least, I thought I did!"*
>
> *She paused.*
>
> *"But then things started to fall apart... I was constantly tired and uncomfortably overweight. I had accepted headaches and insomnia as part of my daily routine. My health was in*

the gutter, and my relationships – well, they were basically non-existent; I barely saw my friends. Everything I cared about was slipping away."

Sarah's voice softened as she recounted the turning point.

"The wake up call came during a major presentation. My vision blurred, my head was spinning, and I nearly fainted in front of everyone. It was awful. That moment forced me to face reality: I was burning out!"

She leaned back in her chair with a thoughtful smile.

"I realized I just could not keep living like that. My capacity was tapped out. Success was not about doing more, but about doing more of what really matters. So, I made some big changes. I said no to non-essential tasks, set boundaries to protect my personal time, and made self-care a priority."

Sarah's transformation was remarkable.

"I got back into working out again, found time for meditation, and reconnected with friends and family. I even started painting – something I hadn't done in years! I was rediscovering parts of myself I had lost."

Her eyes lit up as she shared the impact of those changes.

"My health improved, my energy levels shot up, and I became a better leader. The team noticed the difference, too. Morale went up, creativity blossomed, and we were more productive than ever. It was like a ripple effect. My journey back to balance didn't just save me, it revitalized everyone around me."

I could not help but be inspired by Sarah's story. It was a powerful reminder that sometimes less is more, and true success comes from prioritizing what really matters.

Busyness is absolutely not a badge of honor! Balancing the demands of leadership requires a fundamental shift in perspective. It means acknowledging that self-care isn't selfish but a strategic necessity. When you take care of yourself by tuning up and finding balance, you're better equipped to lead – whether you're leading yourself, your team, or an entire organization.

Refueling your fire

In Chapter 1, we explored the six rungs on the Energy Ladder of Impact. If you're not quite where you want to be on that ladder, it is time to refuel and recharge so you can get back to full capacity.

Here are some powerful strategies for addressing the red flags we identified earlier. These strategies will help recharge your energy and keep you soaring.

IF…	DO THIS:
Your memory is getting worse…	Start paying attention to when you lose your train of thought. It could be a sign you've got too much on your plate and you might need to slow down and give your brain a breather. Embrace mindfulness practices to keep your mind sharp.
Your diet and digestion are off…	Pay attention to what you eat. Swap those empty-calorie snacks for nutrient-rich food that actually nourish you. Your gut and overall well-being will thank you. Keep your body fueled right, and you'll be ready to conquer whatever comes your way.

TUNE UP

IF...	DO THIS:
You're not drinking enough water...	Upping your water intake is an easy fix that can make a big difference. Make a conscious effort to drink more water throughout the day. Besides feeling more hydrated, it will also help with the effects of stress on your body. So, grab a water bottle and keep it filled – you'll be amazed how much better you feel.
Your sleep is messed up...	Incorporate short energy breaks throughout your day to keep you recharged. For better sleep, start by limiting screen time before bed. Establish a calming bedtime routine. Over the years, I have found deep breathing, a short meditation, or relaxing yin yoga helps me release the chaos of the day and prepare for restful sleep.
You're getting frequent colds and unexplained headaches...	Paying attention to your physical health is key. To help combat these issues, start by incorporating stress-reducing activities into your daily routine. Regular movement and exercise are fantastic ways to manage stress over time. You'll alleviate your current symptoms and build resilience for the future.
You've lost your mojo...	Firstly, book a health checkup with your healthcare provider and make sure there is no underlying medical issue. Rewire your fire by reconnecting with what you love. Set aside time for hobbies and activities that bring you joy. Sometimes, a change in routine can help reignite enthusiasm. Pay attention to your emotional health and seek professional support when needed.

Aligning with your circadian rhythm

Alright, we've talked about how your mindset, mood and

motivation are crucial for keeping your energy tank full. Now, let's dive into what ties it all together: your circadian rhythm.

The circadian rhythm is the body's natural clock that keeps everything running smoothly. It tells you when to wake up, eat, and sleep. It helps regulate your mood and energy levels throughout the day. Ever feel jet-lagged after crossing time zones? That's your circadian rhythm getting thrown off balance. But here's the kicker: you can feel that same jet-lagged grogginess even if you haven't travelled anywhere. Day-to-day life, with its irregular schedules and constant demands, can knock your circadian rhythm out of sync just as easily.

Let's check out the benefits of tuning into our circadian rhythm.

- **Quality rest**: Disrupting your circadian rhythm can mess with your sleep, making you feel groggy and unfocused. Keeping a consistent sleep schedule helps you get the restorative rest you need.

- **Better health**: A well-regulated circadian rhythm supports your overall health, reducing the risk of chronic conditions such as obesity and depression.

- **Peak performance**: Aligning your activities with your circadian rhythm can make you a productivity powerhouse. Find the times throughout the day that you are most alert and energetic, and schedule your most energy-demanding activities during those times.

Here are a few simple tips for syncing up with your circadian rhythm:

- **Eat smart**: Have your meals at regular times and avoid heavy meals late at night. When you eat well, your metabolism thrives, building up your energy stores.

- **Create a sleep sanctuary**: Keep your bedroom cool, dark, quiet, and device-free to create a sleep environment that promotes better rest. Go to bed and wake up at the same time every day to establish consistency that reinforces the natural rhythm.

- **Soak up the sun**: Get plenty of natural light during the day, especially in the morning. Light exposure helps set your natural clock.

By understanding, respecting, and tuning into your circadian rhythm, you are not just optimizing your energy; you are maximizing it. This rhythm is the master conductor of your body's orchestra, ensuring everything plays in harmony.

So, tune up your body's natural rhythm and trust it to guide you to a more energized and balanced life – your vitality depends on it.

Remember, your vitality is the foundation of your ability to thrive, lead, and impact others. I know I am repeating myself, but prioritizing self-care isn't selfish – it's a strategic choice that enhances your leadership and well-being. Embrace these practices, listen to your body, and watch as you transform into a more vibrant, effective, unstoppable version of yourself. Your journey to peak vitality is in your hands!

Vibe, Value, Voice, and Visibility

Now that we have explored the importance of managing vitality, let's dive into the other four igniters that make up your Sparkability Factor: your vibe, your value, your voice, and your visibility.

Remember, these other four key elements are crucial for leading with energy, but they cannot thrive without vitality.

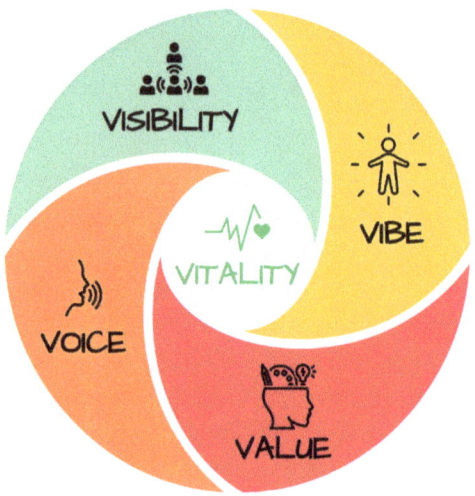

Vibe

Your vibe is the essence of who you are, the unique energy you carry with you and bring to every room, every interaction, and every moment of your life. It is the spark that sets you apart and makes you, well, *you*.

Your vibe is like an ever-burning fire that effortlessly oozes from your pores without you even knowing it. It's that juicy intangible spirit that flows from you, making you a people magnet who subliminally attracts people into your circle of influence.

Your vibe carries a sense of vulnerability and authenticity. Tuning into it involves recognizing your unique qualities and using them in a way that benefits both yourself and others. Bringing your vibe to something means leaving your fingerprints all over it.

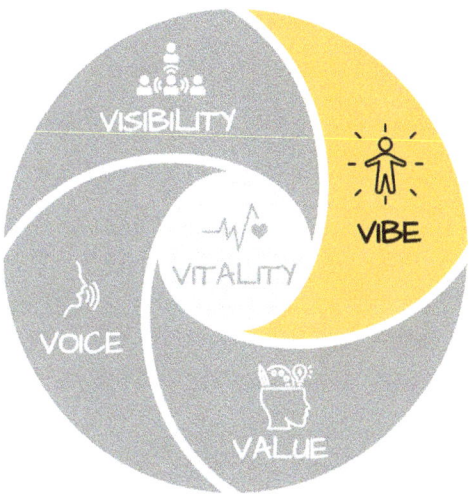

Tuning into your vibe is a process. Sometimes, that process looks like a forest of small children...

> *I was barely 10 years old. It was before the complexities of adulthood had clouded my perceptions. I found myself in a drama class being presented with a simple yet profound challenge by our teacher, Ms. Turner.*
>
> *"Okay class, please spread out and make sure you have plenty of room around you."*
>
> *We scattered and filled the room with excited whispers, awaiting our next instructions.*
>
> *"Okay... quiet, please."*
>
> *We were all still talking, so she repeated herself, this time a little louder.*

"I said quiet, please!

"Ready?

"Pretend you are a tree!"

There was a brief pause as we digested our instructions.

Without holding back, I let my imagination run wild; no limits, no holding back. I could feel my feet rooting deep into the earth, transforming into a strong, solid trunk. I stretched my arms out slightly above shoulder level, allowing them to grow into graceful branches, reaching for the skies. My fingers became delicate leaves that rustled in an imaginary breeze.

Ms. Turner smiled.

"Great, everyone! Well done. Now, hold your position and have a look around the room."

We did our best to hold steady as we peered around the forest of wobbly ten-year-olds. A few giggles escaped the canopy. The children around me stood with their feet firmly planted. They were rooted like trees, but I was unconvinced. Was motionlessness enough to transform them into towering oaks or graceful willows?

"Now, kids, I want you all to relax and turn to look at Kafi."

Oh crap, I thought, What have I done now? She said 'Be a tree,' right? This is a tree!

I held my position and closed my eyes, waiting for an earful.

"Kafi, well done on truly putting yourself into being a tree."

At the time, I didn't fully grasp the significance of her words. But

TUNE UP

Your vibe speaks louder than your voice.

looking back, I recognize the childhood activity for what it was: a glimpse of what it meant to infuse myself into the moment. I didn't *mimic* a tree; I *became* a towering tree.

Likewise, the process of tuning up involves breathing life into your soul to amplify your personal vibe. This can be broken into three steps: define, discover, and infuse.

Step 1: Define

First, you need to define what your personal vibe is. This is about understanding the core values, passions, and qualities that make you unique. To do this effectively, you must also identify and challenge any limiting beliefs that might be holding you back. Left unresolved, those beliefs could hinder your ability to tune into, recognize, and embrace your full self. Questions to contemplate include:

- Who are you?
- What do you stand for?
- What drives you?
- What's your superpower, your 'X' factor, that special sauce that sets you apart?
- What impact do you want to have on the world?
- What do you believe is possible?
- What negative beliefs do you hold about yourself that impact your decisions and actions?
- What positive new beliefs can you adopt to replace the limiting old ones?
- What values are non-negotiable for you?

Step 2: Discover

Next, discover how your vibe manifests in your daily life. This is about understanding your personality traits, the characteristics of your thoughts, feelings, and emotions that impact how you show up and interact with others, the energy you bring to your work, and the way you respond to different situations. It's about peeling back the layers of cultural conditioning, expectations, and past lived experiences. Tuning into your vibe means discovering what the best version of you looks like and stepping into that identity. Some questions to contemplate include:

- Are you an introvert, an extrovert, or somewhere in between (an ambivert)?
- Are you bringing your best self forward or are there areas where you can shine brighter?
- Are you making choices and embracing habits that reflect your true self and the identity you aspire to?

Step 3: Infuse

Finally, infuse your vibe in everything you do. This is where you take that defined and discovered energy and let it permeate every aspect of your life. It's about infusing your personal vibe into your work, your relationships, and your daily routines.

Defining and discovering your personal vibe takes some serious introspection, but infusing it in everything you do? That takes courage—the courage to be authentic and vulnerable. When you show up as your true self, you connect with others on a deeper level and with genuine confidence and empathy.

Make intentional choices that reflect and amplify your unique energy, and watch how your vibe elevates your own experiences and transforms the experiences of those around you.

Again, here are some questions to think about:

- How is your personal vibe influencing the people around you?
- Are your actions aligned with your core values and beliefs?
- How can you show up authentically and embrace vulnerability to build trust and connection with others?
- What steps are you taking to make sure your energy positively impacts your environment?
- Are you being true to yourself or putting on a mask to meet the expectations of others?

By defining, discovering, and infusing your personal vibe into your energy, you create powerful, authentic, magnetic presence that resonates with others. Embrace these steps to tune into a vibe that enables you to lead with energy and create ripples of impact.

The masks we wear

We've all been there, caught between who we are and who we think we should be. Cultural programming, societal pressures, and our own fears push us to wear masks that hide our true essence.

These masks are like little prisons, stifling and restrictive. They create unintentional barriers between you and others, which in turn lead to miscommunication and mistrust.

Imagine shedding your masks like old, uncomfortable clothes. It feels liberating, doesn't it? Being authentically yourself is the key to unlocking this freedom. Infusing the essence of who you are into your approach is like stepping into the perfect fit. You breathe easier, think more clearly, and lead with unwavering confidence.

Consider how it feels to talk with someone who is guarded,

restrained, and constantly calculating their words. On the other hand, how does it feel to talk with someone genuine, open, and unafraid to show their true self? At the center of our most connected, transparent, trusting relationships, we find authenticity.

Now, authenticity isn't about being loud, brash, or braggadocious; it's about giving yourself permission to shine as you lead with true essence. In this state, you're not constantly second-guessing your actions or words. You're not worrying about maintaining a facade. You are navigating with magnetic confidence because you're grounded in authenticity.

Your authenticity encourages others to embrace their own uniqueness and unleash their potential (remember Amani on the dancefloor?). Consider the leaders who have inspired you the most. Were they afraid to show their true selves, warts and all? Unlikely! You become an inspiration when you tune in and infuse with your vibe.

Your vibe speaks louder than your voice

Our vibe speaks volumes. Like a Wi-Fi signal, it is always broadcasting. Strong or weak, negative or positive, it impacts everyone in range and reminds us to be mindful of the energy we radiate.

People feel your vibe before they hear your voice, so make sure your energy does the talking long before you open your mouth.

Later in this chapter, we'll explore using the power of your voice to amp up your energy so that when you speak, you pack an even bigger punch, but let's not get ahead of ourselves. For now, let's continue laying the groundwork for your Sparkability Factor.

Value

Alright, you've nailed your personal vibe and how to let it shine in everything you do. Now, let's kick it up a notch. We're going to dive into another key igniter of your Sparkability Factor that makes you truly invaluable: your value.

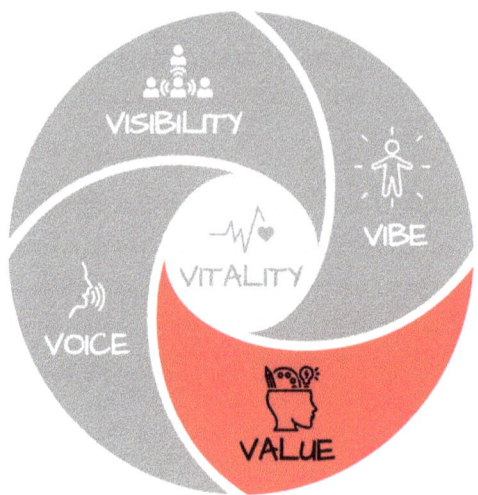

Your value is about knowledge, expertise, skills, and the secret sauce that makes you irreplaceable. When you embrace and showcase your true worth, you boost your own confidence and open the door to inspiring and influencing everyone around you. So, let's find out how you can uncover and leverage the value you bring to the table.

The power of expertise

Okay, let's get into the nitty-gritty.

You might think of expertise as simply knowing stuff. And sure, that's part of it! But there's a whole lot more beneath the surface.

Think of your expertise as the operating system of the latest smartphone. It's not just about the phone's sleek design or the apps and functionalities that make it truly powerful; it's about knowing how to navigate those features so you can actually put them to good use when it counts.

Case in point: a few years ago, my 85-year-old father insisted on getting the latest mobile phone model with all the bells and whistles, but, as much as the family tried to teach him, he only ended up using it to make and receive calls.

Here's the deal: having the best information and tools means nothing if you don't know how to use them. Just like my dad's phone, your expertise can be totally underutilized if you don't know how to master it, nurture it, and make it work for you.

Expertise is not just about what you know; it's about how you use your modern-day operating system to stand out and shift others forward. Let's explore the incredible shifting power of your expertise.

From information to wisdom

The S-shaped curve below symbolizes growth and progression in relation to expertise.

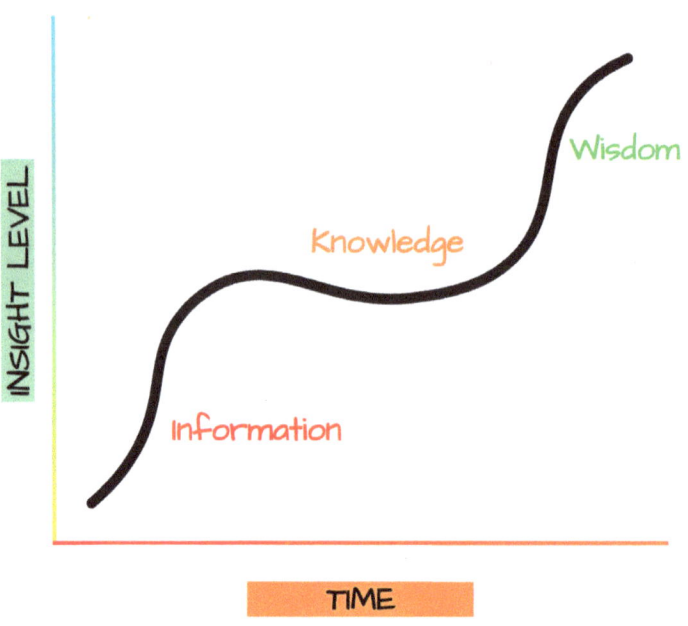

It starts with *Information*. This is the stage where data, facts, and details live. It's the base of the curve – the solid foundation for learning. Think of it as having a pile of puzzle pieces spread out on a table. While each piece is essential, it's just the beginning of the journey. The real magic happens when you start putting the pieces together.

As you move up from Information, you reach *Knowledge*.

At this stage, random facts come together to form a clear picture. This is where you apply what you know in meaningful ways. Knowledge turns isolated pieces of information into something useful, laying the ground for deeper understanding and insight.

The most intriguing part of this journey lies at the curve's peak: *wisdom. Here*, we find a mature perspective and profound insights.

Wisdom emerges from reflecting on knowledge, applying it to life's experiences, and deeply aligning yourself with the content you have.

When you reach wisdom, you have not only assembled the puzzle but gained an intimate understanding of the image it created. Wisdom is the realization that the puzzle incorporates the complexities of life. If some pieces are missing, that's totally okay because it is about embracing the beauty of the incomplete. Wisdom represents what you know and the insights drawn from your lived experiences.

The art of leading with energy involves sharing expertise and wisdom. But it's not about preaching; it's about weaving stories that touch the hearts and minds of others. This is how you'll transform your expertise into a dynamic tool for leading with energy. But before sharing our wisdom through expression and storytelling, we must first learn how to tune into and capture it.

Start with information

Most of us rely on tools like resumes, certificates of accomplishment, and awards to demonstrate what we know. We also hold a zillion other memories about what we know between our ears.

I have so much stuff catalogued in my brain, I don't always do the best job of accessing, searching, and extracting what I need at the right times. After decades of filing in my head, things are a little cluttered in this grey matter of mine. One of the things my friend and master mentor, Col Fink, says is be sure to capture and catalog thoughts and experiences so they are accessible, searchable, and retrievable, quickly and efficiently.

One of the tools I use to get out of my head and capture my

personal and professional lived experiences is a timeline exercise. It goes like this:

Step 1: Reflect and list

Start by taking a trip down memory lane. Reflect on your past experiences, both professional and personal. Think about the challenges you've overcome, the projects you've nailed, and the skills you've picked up along the way.

- **Grab a notebook**: Write down everything you can think of. No filter, no judgement, just let it flow.
- **Focus on wins**: Highlight your achievements and the skills you used to get there. This is not the time to be modest – own your victories!
- **Include everything**: Technical skills, unique talents, personal accomplishments... if it's part of your repertoire, it belongs on the list.

Step 2: Organize and visualize

Now that you've got a massive list of your badassery, it's time to organize it. Categorize your skills and knowledge into areas of expertise, then create a timeline to visualize your growth and development.

- **Create categories**: Group similar skills together (leadership, communication, technical expertise, etc.).
- **Rank and prioritize**: Identify your top strength and note any skills you want to develop further.

TUNE UP

- **Timeline exercise**: Draw a timeline of your career, marking significant milestones and achievements. Reflect on patterns and growth over time.

Here is a snapshot of the timeline I share with clients to give them a sense of how it all comes together.

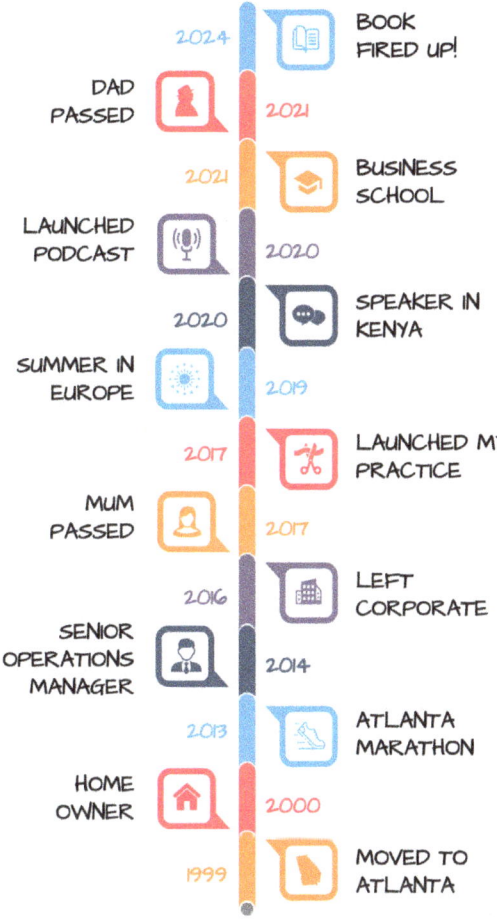

Step 3: Capture and showcase

Make your expertise and skills accessible and searchable by creating a system that you regularly update and showcase.

- **Build a testimonial portfolio**: Collect samples of your work. This could be reports, presentations… anything that shows you in action. Also, collect praises and good vibes that come from others (sidenote: I failed to do this during my two-plus decades as a management consultant, and it later burnt me in the butt!).

- **Establish a digital inventory**: Use a digital tool like Evernote, Notion or a spreadsheet to create a searchable on-going list of skills that you can search and access when needed.

By capturing and cataloging your skills, you create a powerful tool from which you can leverage information whenever you need it.

Next, let's take all that information and turn it into wisdom.

Shift to wisdom

Speaker, author, and mentor, Matt Church, always asks, "Do you want to be known as a thought repeater or a thought leader?"

Of course, we want to be the latter, but the real question is, *how do you go from spewing information to imparting true wisdom?* Here's the juice:

Step 1: Understand the context

- **Read the room**: Know your audience and the situation. Tailor your knowledge to fit the context. What do they need to know? What's relevant right now?

TUNE UP

By shifting from sharing information to imparting wisdom, you're not just a knowledge bearer, you're a guide, a mentor, and a rockstar leader. You're helping others not just learn, but understand, apply, and grow.

- **Connect the dots**: Use your knowledge to draw connections between concepts. Show how different pieces of information relate to each other and to the bigger picture.

Step 2: Immerse Yourself

- **Solve problems**: Use your knowledge to address specific challenges or questions. Offer actionable solutions and insights that others can apply immediately.

- **Be relatable**: Turn theory into practice. Share personal anecdotes and stories that illustrate your points. People connect with stories because stories make knowledge come alive.

- **Share highlights, lowlights, and insights**: Focus on the lessons you've learned from your experiences. What worked? What didn't? How did you grow from these experiences?

Step 3: Seek wisdom sharers and stay humble

- **Ask questions**: Encourage others to think critically about the information at hand. Ask open-ended questions that prompt reflection and deeper understanding.

- **Share for growth**: Highlight the importance of ongoing growth and learning. Always give credit where credit is due. Share resources, books, or courses that might help others expand their knowledge and wisdom.

- **Stay humble**: Be approachable and share your knowledge without coming across as a know-it-all. Wisdom is about helping people, not showing off. Be open to learning from others – a wise person knows everyone has something to share.

By shifting from sharing information to imparting wisdom, you're not just a knowledge bearer; you're a guide, a mentor, and a rockstar leader. You're helping others not just learn, but understand, apply, and grow. Sure, knowledge is power, but leveraging it? That's where true value and worth come into play. By understanding your strengths and continually growing, you can transform raw information into game-changing wisdom. This is how you boost your energy, elevate your worth and tap into your value – the third igniter of your Sparkability Factor.

Voice

Alright, now that we understand how to turn knowledge into wisdom and share it with humility, let's talk about another important igniter of your Sparkability Factor – your voice. Your voice is not just a means of communication; it's a powerful, dynamic instrument that energizes and inspires those around you.

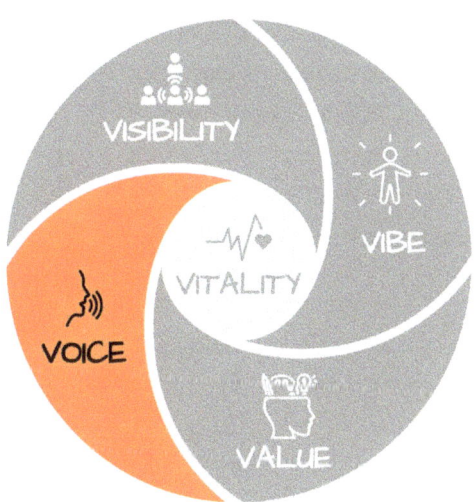

Imagine standing on stage at a major conference. The audience is waiting, the spotlight is on you, and the atmosphere is charged with anticipation. As a speaker, you have the power to captivate the crowd, set the tone, and lead them on a journey of discovery and inspiration. Your voice takes center stage.

In any setting where you influence or lead others, your voice is your stage presence. It's the power that carries your message, the script that drives your impact and the thread that connects those around you on a journey of highs and lows. The words you choose and the way you deliver them determine whether your audience is engaged and inspired or lost and disconnected.

Here's a startling fact: on an average workday, the average person speaks about 16,000 words.[16] And that's just an ordinary day! As leaders, our word count skyrockets even further! Every phrase we utter has the potential to shape the perceptions, decisions, and successes of those in our circle of influence. But it's not just about the quantity of our words; it's about the quality.

What you say has a significant impact on how your message is received, but how you say it also matters. To get our messages across clearly and energetically, we cannot rely solely on choosing the right words; we must also consider tone, context, and the audience's needs and expectations.

Let's rewind to a pivotal moment in my early career. My then-boss, let's call him Joe, was addressing a group of aspiring leaders. We were all part of a company going through fast growth. Joe was priming some of us for new leadership positions to absorb some of the fast growth. Like me, he'd been plucked from the UK to work in the US. He was a good manager and exactly what was needed to grow the US portion of the business.

In any setting where you influence or lead others, your voice is your stage presence. It's the power that carries your message, the script that drives your impact and the thread that connects those around you on a journey of highs and lows. The words you choose and the way you deliver them determine whether your audience is engaged and inspired or lost and disconnected.

Joe did not mince words. He spoke his mind at *all* times.

He had called a meeting to gather a dozen or so of us senior consultants. We sat around a large conference table in our Houston office.

As he was outlining the company's growth strategy for the coming year, he addressed the team.

"Alrighty," he said, "it's time to step up! But if you screw up, you're out. You heard me! I said, *if you screw up, you are out!*"

What the crap? I couldn't believe my ears. Yes, I very much wanted to play the leadership game, but damn you, Joe, thanks for putting the fear of the universe in me – I was about ready to grab my purse and bolt out the door! A bit dramatic, I know, but this is not what I signed up for!

That moment taught me that leadership is not merely about issuing orders or making decisions; it's about understanding the power of words and the subtleties (or not-so-subtleties) of communication. It's about weaving a narrative that inspires, empowers, and connects.

Finding your voice in a noisy world

By using your voice effectively, you can create a positive ripple effect that energizes and inspires others. Your voice has the power to lift spirits, ignite passions, and drive action. So, embrace this tool with confidence and let your words make a difference. Whether you're leading a team, giving a presentation, or having a one-on-one conversation, use your voice to spread your unique energy and inspire those around you.

Let's explore three ways you can tune in to find your own voice.

TUNE UP

1. **Speak with purpose:**
   - **Be clear and concise.** Just like a speaker who crafts a compelling talk, ensure your message is clear and to the point. Avoid unnecessary jargon and get straight to the heart of what you want to convey.
   - **Know your why.** Understand the purpose behind your words. Are you trying to inspire, inform, or motivate? Having a clear intention will make your message more powerful.

2. **Use your vocal energy:**
   - **Inject passion.** Let your enthusiasm shine through your words. People are drawn to energy, and when you speak with genuine excitement, it's contagious.
   - **Modulate your tone.** A skilled speaker uses variations in tone, volume, and pace to keep the audience engaged. A dynamic delivery can make your message more compelling and memorable.

3. **Connect emotionally:**
   - **Tell stories.** Personal anecdotes and stories are powerful tools for connection. They make your message relatable and help others see your human side.
   - **Show empathy.** Listen actively and respond with empathy. Show that you understand and care about your audience's feelings and perspectives.
   - **Be authentic.** Speak from the heart and be true to yourself. Authenticity builds trust and makes your message more impactful.

What you say matters

As someone people look to, the language you use can either light up the room or suck the energy right out of it. High-energy leaders know how to inspire and connect using positive, powerful words. Equally, low-energy leaders can unintentionally flip the script, creating doubt and disengagement. Here are a few side-by-side examples to show how words can make all the difference.

Low-Energy Words	High-Energy Words
"How the heck are we going to handle this?"	"What's our game plan to crush this challenge head-on?"
"Let's stick with the old way. There's no point in messing with something that's already working!"	"Let's trust our tried-and-tested solution. Our expertise will carry us to the next level!"
"What's the point of doing this, anyway?"	"Let's weigh the benefits of giving this a real shot."
"I'm concerned about how this might play out."	"Let's dive into this so we can move forward with confidence."

See the difference? Using high-energy words flips the script from problems to possibilities, encouraging a proactive and positive approach that empowers your message. When you swap out dull for dynamic, you are not just talking – you are commanding attention, inspiring action, and making sure your message lands with impact.

When you own the full power of your voice – through the words you choose, the tone you set, and the energy you project, you are not just communicating; you are leveling up your presence. This is what raises your Sparkability Factor!

Visibility

Alright, we've covered vitality, vibe, value, and the power of your voice. Now let's tune into the final element of your Sparkability Factor: visibility. Remember those masks we wore to fit in, to avoid standing out, or to protect ourselves from judgment? Well, it's time to ditch them and embrace the power of being seen.

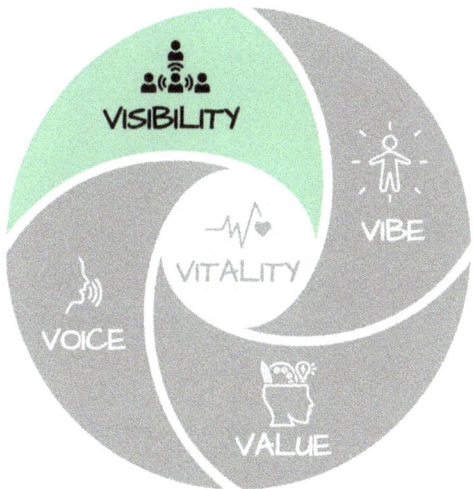

Visibility is not just about being noticed; it's about being fully self-expressed, being authentically you, and showing up with all your unique awesomeness. Think of Amani, moving her happy little hips on the dance floor. When you allow yourself to take up space and be fully seen, you inspire others to do the same, creating a ripple of authenticity and connection.

The fear of being seen

Lots of people know how to stand out and be effective, but the fear of being seen and judged holds them back. Instead of letting that fear run the show, flip your mindset and focus on the positive impact you can have on others.

Use your visibility to create positive relational energy and step into the spotlight with confidence. Rather than dwelling on the fear of judgment, ask yourself, "How can my visibility illuminate others?"

This shift in perspective allows you to see your presence as a force for good, inspiring and uplifting those around you. Your visibility isn't just about you, it's about the energy you bring to your interactions and the positive ripples you can set in motion.

Own your presence

As leaders, we often find ourselves shrinking back, doubting our worth, and feeling like we need to fit into a smaller box to make others comfortable. It's time to give yourself permission to take up space. Here's how:

- **Show up fully**. Be 100% present in every face-to-face interaction you have (whether in person or in a virtual environment). Make eye contact, listen actively, and engage genuinely. Your presence is powerful, and when you show up fully, you command attention and respect.

- **Radiate confidence**. Walk into every room with your head held high. Stand tall, speak clearly, and own your space. Confidence is magnetic; it draws people towards you.

- **Be authentic**. I've said it before, I'll say it again – authenticity is your superpower. Be yourself, flaws and all. People connect

TUNE UP

When you speak, let your enthusiasm and passion shine through. Positive emotions are contagious and can elevate the mood and energy of everyone in the room.

with genuine energy, and your authenticity will inspire others to be real too.

- **Focus on the energy exchange.** Your presence, words, and actions all contribute to the vibe in the room. Aim to make this energy a positive force. By doing so, you not only alleviate your own fears but also enhance the experience for everyone else involved.

Embrace your role as CEO

As a leader, you hold the title of 'Chief Energy Officer.' You're an energy catalyst who not only brings their best self to the table but also elevates the energy of those around them. Focus on the energy exchange. When you speak, let your enthusiasm and passion shine through. Positive emotions are contagious and can elevate the mood and energy of everyone in the room.

Foster an inclusive environment by encouraging others to share their thoughts and ideas. This not only empowers them but also creates a dynamic and energetic atmosphere. Lead by example. Show resilience in the face of challenges, optimism in the face of uncertainty, and kindness in all interactions. Your behavior sets the tone for others to follow.

Elevate the room

Using your visibility as an energy catalyst means lifting the energy of the entire room, whether you are one-to-one or one-to-many. Small wins that will give you big impact include:

- **Leading with positivity.** Your energy sets the tone. Enter the room with a positive attitude and a smile. Positivity is infectious and can transform the atmosphere instantly.

- **Engaging enthusiastically**. Show enthusiasm in your interactions. Whether it's a meeting, a presentation, or a casual conversation, your enthusiasm will energize those around you.

- **Acknowledging others**. Recognize and appreciate the contributions of others. A simple acknowledgment can boost someone's energy and create a ripple effect of positivity.

By shifting your mindset from fear to positive impact, you transform your approach to visibility. If you focus on creating positive relational energy, you'll find it easier to step up and be seen. Your presence, words, and actions all have the power to uplift and inspire. Embrace this power to let your authentic self shine, and make a positive difference in every interaction.

Your presence and the space you take up in the world matter!

So, tuning up is the first part of the Fired Up! Framework. How you tune up is anchored by your Sparkability Factor. The five igniters (vitality, vibe, value, voice and visibility) are all connected in one powerful energy-boosting loop. Your vitality fuels your personal vibe, which in turn, elevates your sense of value. Embracing your worth and sense of value gives strength to your voice, and using your voice powerfully, amplifies your visibility. It's all about raising your energy, owning your power and letting that ripple out in everything you do. When the elements are in sync, and you give yourself permission to shine, you're unstoppable!

Key Takeaways

1. The Fired Up! Framework is how we lead with energy. It's a guide for optimizing your energy, exploring and assessing the energy of others, and then shifting the group's energy (yours and theirs) to where you want it to be. It has three parts: *Tune Up*, *Sync Up*, and *Lift Up*.

2. This chapter focuses on tuning up. It's about maximizing your Sparkability Factor—your ability to shift and lift the vibe of others.

3. Sparkability Factor is fueled by five igniters: your vitality, vibe, value, voice, and visibility.

4. **Your vitality** is at the core of your Sparkability Factor—the lifeblood of energetic leadership that dictates how you show up for others. Tap into your mindset, mood, and motivation to amplify your capacity to manage stress, build resilience and reduce burnout.

5. **Your vibe** speaks louder than your voice. Take off the mask and give yourself permission to shine.

6. Knowing and embracing your worth is not about being boastful; it is about standing out in a crowded market with confidence and authenticity. When you truly understand **your value**, resist the urge to be a smartass. Instead, turn it into something that makes a real difference for others. It is about recognizing your skills, experience and expertise, and flipping that information and knowledge into wisdom that serves others. Move from just having information to using it like a pro and leverage your lived experiences to create undeniable value.

TUNE UP

7. **Your voice** is a powerful tool. What you say and how you say it matters! Use the full power of your voice –choose your tone and inflection, and trade those weak, low-energy words for high-energy words that light up the room and empower your message. When you own the energy behind your voice, you amplify your message ensuring it resonates deeply and leaves a lasting impact.

8. Overcome your fear of being seen and amplify **your visibility** by boldly stepping into the spotlight where you belong. Embrace the role of an energy catalyst or better yet, become the Chief Energy Officer by using your vibrant energy to elevate the vibe of a space whether you're one-on-one or addressing a crowd.

Vibe Shifters

Use the following prompts to help put your chapter insights into action.

Vitality:

1. What would have to happen for you to feel more energized on a regular basis?
2. What activities make you feel tired and sluggish?
3. What type of diet gives you the most consistent energy?
4. What are you currently doing in life (or work) that is consistently lighting you up and giving you energy?
5. List three things that are causing you to leak energy and explain how the energy drain affects you day-to-day?
6. What daily practices do you use to manage your stress and well-being?

Vibe:

7. What are you excited about? What fills you with joy and purpose?
8. With the understanding that your vibe speaks louder than your voice - what does your vibe say about you?
9. What are your top three personal values and why is each one important to you?

Value:

10. What are you amazingly great at that most people struggle with?

11. What is the top compliment you receive the most?

12. What are you super enthusiastic about that you wish more people shared a passion for?

Voice:

13. What keywords or phrases are you frequently using when communicating with others?

14. Are your words energizing and uplifting or draining and demoralizing?

15. How would you like to use your voice to influence others and create positive impact in the world?

Visibility:

16. If you gave yourself permission to brag unapologetically, what would you brag about?

17. How are you showing up in the world? Are you hiding and playing small or letting yourself be seen?

18. What is the story you are telling yourself about visibility and how can you rewrite it to empower yourself?

19. If you were not worried about what people think, how would you show up differently in work and life?

For additional resources related to spark-ability, head to kafilondon.com/firedup or scan the QR Code and follow the **Resources** link.

kafilondon.com/firedup

CHAPTER SIX

Sync Up

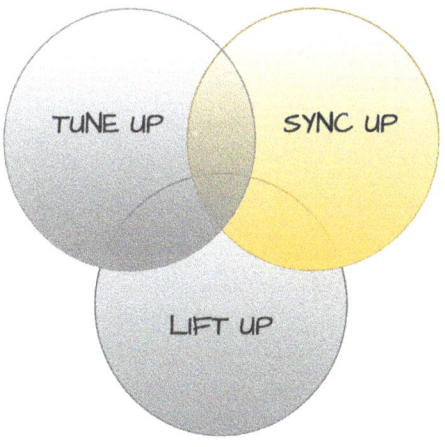

Taking the time to focus in and sync up with others before you let yourself loose energetically gives you a powerful advantage. When leaders skip this step, it always ends badly because they lack key information. Syncing up can be the difference between connecting seamlessly versus missing the mark entirely.

When I lead spin classes, there is a critical point at the beginning of the ride where I consciously scan from rider to rider. As I do, I pick up subtle cues that provide the insight I need to tailor that particular experience; I then adjust my coaching style to create an experience that connects and challenges everyone.

Often, when we are feeling aspirational and excited about stepping into a leading role, we can simply forget we are leading others. We end up on tangents, losing sight of the very people we intended to serve. It's not intentional, it just seems to happen. I know because I am also guilty of doing this when I focus more on sharing what I know than on serving those in front of me.

In Chapter Five, we focused on tuning up by checking in with our vitality, vibe, value, voice and visibility. Syncing up requires us to tune in to the Sparkability Factor of others. We need to be in sync with them if we aspire to lead them.

An amateur move is to jump right into serving – we all do it because we are ready to impress and make an impact. The pro move is to assess where they are and how they are feeling before you start your journey together. This requires situational awareness.

Situational awareness is the ability to gather information from your environment, interpret it accurately, and predict potential outcomes. It's about being conscious of what is happening around you and making informed decisions. In a business, it may not seem that important, but in fields such as healthcare and military operations, even driving a vehicle in everyday life, situational awareness is essential for safety and effective decision making.

Taking the time to sync up and read the room gives you a huge advantage, as you will know where those you hope to shift are starting energetically.

My friend and close associate, let's call her April, shared the costly outcome of missing this step in a recent client engagement.

April had spent months working to win a contract with a luxury retail company. Finalizing the contract took a lot more mental and emotional energy than expected, but when she finally got the news that she had won the contract, she realized it had all been worth it.

The client wanted her to deliver her signature workshop to three different departments. April was over-the-moon excited – what a win! As soon as the contractual and procurement elements were finalized and the date of each workshop was agreed to, she shifted into tune-up mode so she was ready, willing and able to deliver her best work.

Fast forward to the day of the first workshop, April was prepped, energized, and raring to go.

However, everything on the client's side was behind schedule. An earlier workshop had over-run, they were likely mentally exhausted, and the last thing they wanted to do was roll right into another workshop.

April sensed the fatigue settling in, so she asked everyone to take a short brisk walk outside for some fresh air to recharge.

A few minutes later, with everyone seated back in the room, April started her workshop and pushed through her content as best she could in the rest of the time that was allotted.

All was well – at least she thought. One workshop down, two to go!

Later that evening, the senior HR rep (who had originally secured April's contract) shared the news that the second and third workshops were cancelled.

> *April was devastated – what happened? What of all the blood, sweat, and work that she'd put into securing the contract?*
>
> *A few weeks later, April bravely talked about her recent situation. On reflection, she realized she had not tapped into the energy of the room. She'd tuned up and was keen to lift up, but she'd skipped the step of syncing up. While she was ready to teach and get through the contracted workshop, the attendees were not "in-state" and ready to receive, so there was a missed connection.*

Taking time to read the room and sync up is empowering. This information helps you gauge where people are energetically in the current moment, giving you the power to adapt your approach. In April's case, she concluded, it could have been the game changer. Having the skills to read the room (and taking the time to actually do so) can significantly affect how others receive you and your point, message, or intention.

Lucky for you, I won't ask you to rely on psychic powers for syncing up (I'm pretty sure I don't have any). Instead, I'll provide you with practical insights and tips that you can apply in any situation, whether you're interacting with people in person, virtually, one-on-one, or in a group setting.

Setting yourself up for success

We have all read rooms. If you have ever been to a party, conference, gym class, family reunion, or leadership retreat, you have read a room before. Whether you are comfortable entering a room of strangers or not, a quick scan of the room can pump you up to dive right in... or make you want to bolt for the door.

SYNC UP

Whether you are walking into a room of strangers, people who already know each other, or a mixed group of individuals, reading a room gives you information about the feeling or vibe of the room. Equipped with this information, you can better connect, engage, and nurture conversations with people.

In 'Reading the Room', author David Kantor breaks it down for us.[17] Kantor says that by understanding the secret sauce of group dynamics, you can totally own the room. He also suggests that whether you are feeling like a Mover, Follower, Opposer or Bystander, knowing your role can turn anxiety into a positive feeling.

Reading a room is not networking. Consider it to be the precursor to engaging with people. Whether you are walking into a room of strangers, people who already know each other, or a mixed group of individuals, reading a room gives you information about the feeling or vibe of the room. Equipped with this information, you can better connect, engage, and nurture conversations with people. The bottom line is: it's difficult for people to invest in our thoughts, ideas, products, or services if we bypass this step and ignore some of the initial signs. The top three benefits you gain from reading a room are summarized in the table below.

IF YOU WANT...	LOOK FOR...	USE THE INFO TO...
Better Communication	Body language, facial expressions, and tone of voice.	Tailor your message to ensure it is properly received.
Increased Engagement	Levels of engagement, reactions, and signs of tension.	Determine the types of interactive activities necessary to build trust and avoid conflict.
Increased Influence	Mood, morale, enthusiasm, and signs of fatigue or tension.	Establish how long you should spend on introductory activities to align everyone.

I am still surprised when clients tell me they don't think about reading a room, or that they simply go straight to icebreaking or some sort of "engagement activity" without having taken the time to check in and sync up first.

But this skill isn't limited to work or leadership; it comes in handy in situations across the board. Most of us want to feel comfortable and be accepted by others, and we usually want to make others feel comfortable with us, too. This is true regardless of the setting.

Salsa dancing is one of my favorite activities. When my regular dance partner, James, is out of town, I still get a little nervous thinking I might end up with a partner who's got no rhythm, stepping on my toes all night, or one so advanced he's got me spinning so fast I'm flung right off the dance floor. So, when my friends and I decide to hit a salsa spot, I always show up early to read the crowd. I scan the room as people pile in.

That person looks fun!

That guy could do with loosening up a little.

Ooooh, they have confident energy!

Yikes, that dude has some back-breaking dips. I'll pass.

Having had the opportunity to read the room and sync up with the other dancers' energies, I feel more at ease about dancing with strangers when the music starts. If I know my partner feels uneasy, I won't come at them all guns blazing (or flinch in surprise when my hands meet their sweaty palms). I'll know to smile reassuringly and keep dancing when they step on my feet. Likewise, if I know my partner feels confident and loose, I can bring bundles of big energy and let them lead. When they step on my feet, I'll feel relaxed about correcting their footwork, knowing they won't be thrown off (these are the dancers I tend to beeline for!).

Giving myself time to sync up means I know who to dart towards when the fiery Latin music starts, and, regardless of who I end up dancing with, the two of us can connect and engage more instantly.

I am not suggesting you get your dance on (not unless that's your thing, of course). I'm suggesting that whatever you're getting into - whether that's a leadership meeting, a house full of teenagers, or a salsa session – there is value in reading the room before diving in at the deep end.

Decoding cues

Okay, Kafi, we get that we need to read a room before diving in, but... how?

Reading a room involves tuning in, observing, and understanding the dynamics, mood, energy, and buzz of a setting.

In her book *'Cues: Master the Secret Language of Charismatic Communication'*, Vanessa Van Edwards emphasizes that knowing how to turn body language and energy cues into actionable insights sets you up for greater influence and impact.[18] You read a room by looking around for cues to decode. This is a skill which comes with practice, but you can start today. Let's jump in.

1. **Observe body language:**

    These cues can reveal what someone is truly feeling. Watch for non-verbal signals like posture, gestures, and facial expressions. Are they leaning in, arms open, and smiling? That's engagement and interest. Crossed arms, avoiding eye contact, or frowning? That's resistance or discomfort.

2. **Listen to tone and pace:**

   The way someone speaks is just as important as what they say. A fast, high-pitched voice can signal excitement or anxiety, while a slow, calm tone might indicate relaxation or confidence. Use this information to adjust your communication style when the time is right.

3. **Notice micro-expressions:**

   These are the tiny, involuntary facial expressions that flash across a person's face for just a fraction of a second. They're like sneak peeks into their true emotions and can provide insights into what they're really feeling.

4. **Pay attention to context:**

   Context is king. The same gesture or tone can mean different things in different settings. What's normal in a casual chat might be totally out of place in a formal meeting, for example. The environment and situation will shape the appropriate response.

5. **Practice active listening:**

   Don't just hear words; listen actively. What do you *really* hear? Tune in and out of near and far conversations as time allows, and extend your hearing past the words. What other ambient sounds fill the room? Is there music playing in the background or noise filtering in from a nearby location that is adding or taking away from the environment?

Whether you are mingling at a party, leading a team meeting or presenting to a crowd, mastering the skill of reading a room and decoding the cues helps you connect at a deeper level. This ability allows you to sync up with others and lead with confidence.

Key Takeaways

1. Sync up is the second part of the Fired Up! Framework.

2. Before you start trying to influence others, sync up to assess where they are.

3. Taking the time to sync up can be the difference between connecting seamlessly versus missing the mark entirely.

4. Syncing up with others involves reading the room – whether you are one-on-one or with many.

5. The top three benefits of reading a room are: better communication, increased engagement, and increased influence.

6. Decoding cues is like being a social detective picking up on all the unspoken signals people are putting out.

Vibe Shifters

Use the following prompts to help put your chapter insights into action.

1. How often do you listen to the energy of what's not being said and pick up on the unspoken cues before diving into action?

2. What's your go-to strategy for reading the vibe of a room?

3. How can you sharpen your go-to strategy to be more effective?

4. Picture yourself as the DJ at a party. How would you tune into the mood and dynamics of the room. What clues would you pick up on to decide what to play next and keep the party rocking?

For additional resources on syncing up and reading the room head to kafilondon.com/firedup or scan the QR code below and follow the **Resources** link.

kafilondon.com/firedup

CHAPTER SEVEN

Lift Up

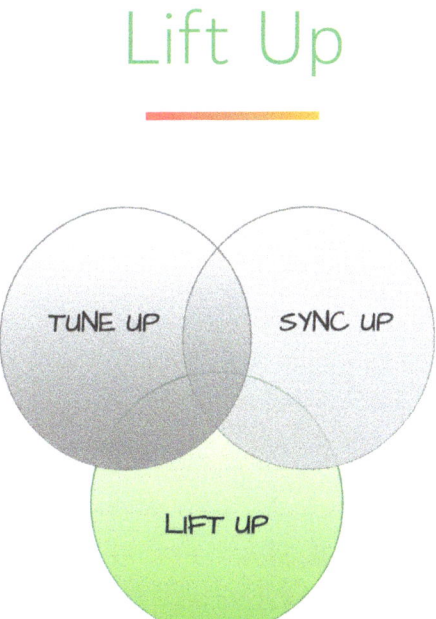

Having tuned up with the five igniters of your Sparkability Factor (vitality, vibe, value, voice, and visibility), you are set up for success when it comes to your own personal energy. We've also discussed ways of syncing up with others, no matter their energy levels.

We're ready for the next level: elevating the energy of others. This is the realization of all our work towards leading with energy. It's a shift that doesn't just happen overnight. Moving from lifting your own energy to lifting others' means building trust and rapport to create space (literally or otherwise) where people feel valued and understood. It's amazing how a bit of empathy and transparency can transform those around you.

Each and every interaction is an opportunity to leave a lasting, positive impression. The moments we share with others are chances to make our connections so meaningful that everyone walks away feeling better than they did before you connected. That is what energizes people and starts the ripple.

Energized and meaningful connections make people feel heard, seen, and appreciated. It is not about getting through a set agenda. By focusing our energy on lifting others, we can turn meetings and gatherings into energizing exchanges that boost morale and drive motivation.

Leading with energy is something I do with unconscious competence (I can do it well without thinking about it). People often compliment my energy and the way I lift theirs, asking, "How can I have some of that?"

I used to find this question hard to answer. In fact, my answers probably came across as if I was hiding something because I didn't really know what I did – I just did it! How could I explain something that happened without conscious thought? Turns out, nine months of fun (but challenging!) improv was all I needed to understand what was going on under the hood.

Lessons from improv

The Whole World Improv Theatre (yes, they spell it this way to be fancy) is led by 30-year improv veteran and Artistic Director Chip Powell. He led me and 15 other improv junkies from all walks of life through many months of improv classes where we discovered the art of being spontaneous. Let's unpack three insights from improv that helped us discover the magic ingredients for bringing people together and elevating the vibe.

1. **Be present and engaged**. This is a non-negotiable in improv. It is all about showing up fully in the moment for both the scene and your scene partner or partners. It's about listening and reacting in real time because there are no scripts to fall back on. This level of presence transforms interactions by ensuring you are genuinely engaged with the people in front of you. Whenever I lost focus, zoned out, or got caught up in my thoughts, Chip busted my butt. I looked like I was engaged in the scene game to an untrained eye, but Chip knew I had lost the connection with my improv partner. As a leader, the lesson is to bring your A-game every time. When you are truly engaged, others see that you are in it with them and that energy pulls everyone together.

2. **Harness Positive Energy.** In improv, the energy you bring can make or break a scene. Picture this: you enter a scene where your partner's energy is neutral, but you make a bold emotional choice – maybe coming in with excitement, urgency, and deep empathy. That choice instantly shifts the dynamic, pulling your partner into a more engaging emotional space, elevating the entire scene. The audience feels the energy shift and the scene comes to life. The same goes for leading others. When you show up with a vibe that is positive, powerful and contagious, you lift others. Your energy sets the tone, so make sure it is the kind that inspires, motivates and keeps the momentum going.

3. **Elevate Others.** In improv, just like in life, sensitivity is your superpower. It's about tuning in, feeling the room, and noticing the subtle cues that let you elevate others around you. During one class, Chip had us step into the role of fearless investigators. Without missing a beat, we stepped into our assigned roles and trusted the magic would be revealed. My scene partners and I didn't just play our parts; we sensed each other's moves, amplified each other's contributions, and made each other shine. As a leader, that's your job — to be sensitive to what others bring to the table, celebrate their brilliance, and make sure every voice is heard and valued. When you lead with sensitivity, you create a culture where everyone feels lifted, connected, and ready to thrive.

These insights from improv class have shown me that forging powerful moments isn't about grand gestures, it's about creating subtle shifts. In our daily lives, it is a collection of small, meaningful micro-moments that ultimately shape our larger experiences.

By focusing on making interactions meaningful, you are not just chatting; you are building a stronger, more connected experience.

Lifting others requires a conscious, consistent effort to engage genuinely, respond constructively, and appreciate openly. If you can get this down, you'll be on the fast track to enhancing individual interactions and building a stronger, more energized group dynamic.

Group gatherings

Whether it is a scheduled daily meeting, game-changing workshop, swanky conference, or bustling community affair, there is power in bringing people together. As Pulitzer Prize-winning

LIFT UP

When you lead with sensitivity, you create a culture where everyone feels lifted, connected, and ready to thrive.

Journalist Garath Cooks explains in his 2013 article in Scientific American, we are wired to connect, share, and grow in the company of others.[19]

In formal settings like meetings, events, workshops, conferences, or corporate retreats, coming together transforms individual insights into collective wisdom. Gatherings are where the lone energy of the right speaker – or group of speakers – can catch fire and ignite the people in the room.

Coming together is not just about sharing knowledge, it's also about evolving and amplifying the vibe and cultivating a sense of belonging. The art of gathering weaves threads of connection into our social fabric. When you realize your job is not just to inform people, but also to inspire, it becomes an opportunity to create a different type of experience that engages and lifts others. When this happens, you change the game and become an outlier.

...But it's not quite as simple as that

Many focus on bringing people together without thinking about anything else. Where? When? Why? How many people? Who? There are many elements involved in a successful gathering.

In 2022, I was the speaker at a corporate event. I went early to check out the room setup and connect with the audio-visual team, but this didn't take long. With some extra time on my hands, I decided to support and enjoy some of the other speakers.

I sat down and joined a session already underway. Over the next few minutes, an uneasiness circled the room. It wasn't anything you could see, but more of a feeling.

The speaker stood rigid behind a lectern, pushing buttons on a keyboard that projected up to a big screen behind them. The room was filled with over two hundred people and, other than the Q&A session, there was no engagement between the presenter and the audience. It felt like a watch-and-listen snooze-fest. Sure, not every presentation needs to be a party, but this was a huge, missed opportunity. With a little effort, they could have sparked some real interaction, made the room come alive and left everyone buzzing. Instead, they lost the chance to connect deeply and make a lasting impact.

This example shows how simply gathering in the same room as other people is not always enough. Of course, every audience, group, meeting or gathering is different, and it's important to adapt your style accordingly. This is a crucial skill in today's diverse work environment. But to do so, your Sparkability Factor must provide a solid foundation to work from. So, let's dive into leveraging that delicious authentic energy you have worked so hard to generate and nurture, and put it into action to lift others up.

Lift others your own way

Everyone has their own style of leadership, and while syncing up with the energy of others is paramount, we must do so without extinguishing our own authentic energy. Lifting others up requires listening and adjusting our styles while keeping our own energy intact.

Let's take a look at two different stories, Jordan's and Lena's, to see this in action.

Jordan

Picture Jordan, a project manager known for his high-octane meetings and tight deadlines. While his methods were effective, he noticed a drop in his team's creative input and enthusiasm. Jordan decided to shift gears, allocating time for listening and engaging with his team's ideas. He started holding 'energy sessions' where team members shared what energized them about their work. These sessions brought new life to the team, leading to innovative solutions and a more engaged workforce. Jordan's journey demonstrates the impact of combining listening with energetic leadership.

Lena

Lena is a tech leader with a more reserved, calm presence. Initially, she worried her quiet energy wasn't enough to inspire her team. However, Lena discovered her strength in empathetic leadership. She created an environment where team members felt heard and valued, leading to a deeply motivated and loyal team. Lena's story is a reminder that energy in leadership isn't just about being loud or outwardly dynamic; it's about the strength and impact of your authentic presence.

These stories show us that it's not just about the energy you bring as a leader; it's about how you channel that energy to focus on those in your circle of influence. By making it about them – their growth, their ideas, their success – you energize your team and amplify your impact as a leader.

Remember, the most effective leaders are those who light a fire in others, not just in themselves. Let's embrace this energizing approach and start lifting others. It's not all about you!

Who are you lifting up?

Before we dive into our approach, let's refer to the Mindset Matrix to break down those we seek to influence and impact into four categories or "character types" based on how they assess and digest information. We've got:

- **Analyzers** – those who crave data and details
- **Creators** – they are constantly pushing the envelope
- **Explorers** – always hungry for new insights
- **Strategists** – they see the big picture and dream big

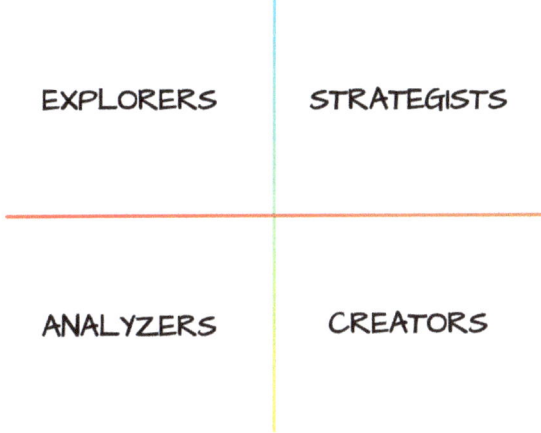

Every character type requires a slightly different approach to get them energized and engaged. Knowing who you are dealing with and tailoring your connection accordingly can make all the difference.

You are responsible for connecting with people wherever they fall in the quadrant, so let's break down how to connect with each group and elevate their energy to create ripples and, eventually, waves of impact.

During my almost three decades in the management consulting industry, my client work was grounded in frameworks. We leveraged Blooms Taxonomy and the ADDIE model. Implicit in these models is the understanding that if the goal is to create learning experiences that are meaningful, motivating, and relevant, we must engage both the cognitive (mind) and emotional (heart) domains. Inspired by Matt Church's work in his book, *Amplifiers*,[20] let's explore the art of creating engaging experiences that shift and lift the vibe further.

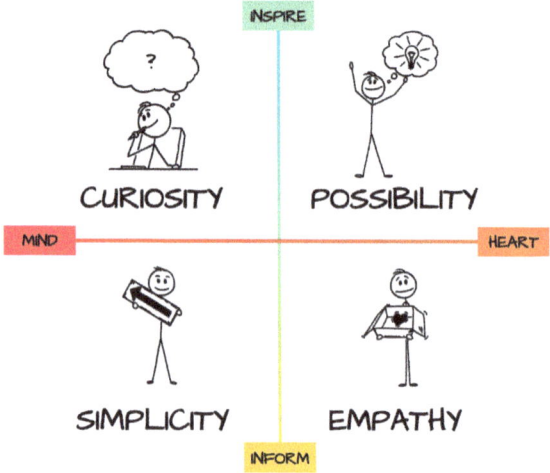

Lifting Analyzers: Inform the mind

These logical thinkers thrive on information, facts, and figures. They crave clarity and logic. They need to understand how all the pieces fit together, and rely on solid data to make decisions. If the information is too complex or unclear, it can lead to confusion and disengagement.

Shift the energy for Analyzers by mastering the art of **simplicity**. Cut through the noise with laser-focused messaging and connect the dots for them. Use straightforward language and avoid jargon to make your message as clear and accessible as possible. Make complex ideas relatable with real-life examples, analogies, and visual aids. These tools help your audience understand and remember your points more easily, keeping things engaging.

Lifting Creators: Inform the heart

The heart-centered Creators thrive on you understanding and acknowledging their feelings and perspectives. To lift, engage and connect with a Creator's energy, start by leading with **empathy**. Make sure your words resonate with them emotionally and are delivered with genuine care and understanding. Establish trust by being transparent, honest, and authentic; this provides the strong emotional connection they need to thrive. Avoid using harsh or judgmental language that can create barriers. Instead, choose words that convey kindness, understanding, and support.

Lifting Explorers: Inspire the mind

Explorers thrive on adventure and a desire to discover new things. They are driven by forward-thinking ideas. Explorers crave intellectual stimulation. Without inspiration, they become disengaged and lose momentum. They need to contribute to the future and how they can shape it.

To effectively inspire Explorers, keep them engaged, and elevate their energy, you need to fuel their **curiosity** and forward-thinking mindset. This means presenting ideas that challenge the status quo and encourage exploration. Address their curiosity by answering "why" and "how" questions. For example, *why is this important?*

and *how will it impact the future?* When you satisfy an Explorer's itch for curiosity, you energize them to reach new heights.

Lifting Strategists: Inspire the heart

Inspired by a sense of intention, Strategists need to feel their work is meaningful and aligned with a greater purpose. Without this, they can become disengaged and lose their drive.

To lift the energy of a Strategist, we need to tap into their passion and ignite their imagination, helping them see the big picture and their role in it. **Possibility** is the tool of choice here—use it to help them see how they can contribute to something greater. Extend the energetic ripple with powerful, heartfelt stories that ignite their passion. Stories of triumph, resilience, and transformation deeply move and inspire Strategists. Encourage them to envision a future where their efforts lead to meaningful change.

The Energy Equation

Once you recognize that your room, space, or situation consists of different character types, elevating the energy in any room, no matter the group size or setting, all comes down to a simple but effective formula:

Powerful Prompts x Engagement Level = Energy Shift!

This energy equation is your secret weapon for transforming ordinary interactions into dynamic, meaningful experiences. By aligning a powerful prompt with the desired level of engagement, you can turn any ordinary conversation, meeting, or large gathering into an experience that energizes, inspires, and connects everyone involved.

LIFT UP

Powerful Prompts x Engagement Level = Energy Shift!

Powerful prompts

Using energizing questions as prompts is a simple and effective way to shift energy. The best questions spark curiosity, ignite creativity, and open fresh perspectives. They're not just conversation starters; they're dynamic gems that pull people out of their heads and into the moment, making them think, share, and connect in ways they didn't see coming. The right question can introduce insights and bold thoughts that bring buzz and excitement to your gathering.

A truly energizing prompt hits the following criteria.

1. **It's open-ended** – it gets people to dig deep and can't be answered with a simple *yes* or *no*.

2. **It's thought-provoking** – it flips the script, pushes people to think outside the box, and might start with "What if…", "How might…", or "Why do you think…" to get the creative juices flowing.

3. **It's relevant and relatable**. Like a mind reader, an energizing prompt taps into current experiences, goals, or challenges, making it feel real and striking in its audience's minds or hearts.

4. **It's emotionally engaging**. The best prompts tap into emotions like curiosity, excitement, empathy, and humor. When people feel something, they can't help but jump in.

5. **It encourages participation** by pulling people in and creating space for more voices, whether from one person, a small group, or a large crowd.

Let's take a look at a few examples of powerful prompts for different settings.

LIFT UP

- **One-to-one (e.g., personal conversations, coaching sessions):**
  - What's the most exciting thing you've been working on lately?
  - If you could change one thing about your current situation, what would it be?
  - What have you always wanted to try?
  - How do you feel about your progress so far, and what's next?
- **Small group (e.g., workshops, team building, small meetings):**
  - What surprising insight have you gained from our recent project?
  - How might we approach this challenge differently as a team?
  - What's one thing we could all do to make this meeting more effective?
  - What strengths do we have within this group that we haven't tapped into yet?
- **Large group (e.g., events, conferences, organizational settings):**
  - What's the boldest idea you've heard recently that could impact our industry?
  - How do you see the future of our field, and what role will we play in it?
  - What would you change about how we currently do things?

- If you could ask our leadership one question, what would it be?

Side note: These are just a few examples of how the right prompt can elevate energy; imagine having a full toolkit of options at your fingertips! If you're struggling to come up with your own energizing questions, don't worry, I got ya! I have created a deck of 60 energizing prompts you can use to shift the energy in any one-on-one, small group or large setting. Go and grab a pack of Spark Cards from kafilondon.com/sparkcards – they'll help you get the ball rolling.

kafilondon.com/sparkcards

Engagement level

With your prompts sorted, we can look at the other part of the equation: engagement level. High-energy questions act as the fuel, but engagement is the amplifier that drives the energy shift.

When you combine powerful prompts with an appropriate level of interaction, whether low engagement (thoughtful responses) or high engagement (enthusiastic participation and lively discussions), you create an atmosphere where people feel more engaged, energized, and invested. That's the sweet spot where curiosity meets engagement, and everyone feels a little more alive.

And here's a pro tip: remember how we talked earlier about

LIFT UP

Add a twist of humor, empathy, or even a touch of challenge, and you'll turn an ordinary gathering into an unforgettable, energy-fueled experience that people will remember.

tuning up your Sparkability Factor — that unique magic only you can bring — and why syncing up helps you sense what's really going on in the room? Are people leaning in, actively listening, or looking a little checked out? Use both of these tools to your advantage. This is your chance to gauge where others are and where you want to take them so your message lands. Decide on the level of engagement you need to create the shift you desire — whether it's starting slow to build trust, creating steady momentum, or going full throttle to ignite high energy.

Add a twist of humor, empathy, or even a touch of challenge, and you'll turn an ordinary gathering into an unforgettable, energy-fueled experience that people will remember.

Low-engagement activities

Low-engagement activities are like wading in the shallow end of the pool — easy-going, no-pressure interactions where participants can dip their toes in and get comfortable without diving in headfirst. These activities create a laid-back vibe, perfect for breaking the ice and setting the stage for more fun. Focus on simple, calming prompts that encourage quiet reflection and help everyone tune into their thoughts and feelings. The goal is to gently raise the energy, allowing participants to warm up and engage at their own pace.

Here are some great low-engagement activities to try:

- **One-to-one**: Invite your partner to quietly reflect on a prompt like "What makes you giggle?" with the option to write down their thoughts, depending on the circumstances. There's no rush to share; just let it marinate and see what bubbles up.

- **Small group**: Introduce a thought-provoking prompt like "What is the compliment you receive most often?" Let everyone reflect silently or jot down their thoughts. Again, there is no need to share. By letting people work through the question in their own way, you create a calm, reflective vibe that gets everyone in a positive headspace.

- **Large group**: Start with an energizing prompt like "If you could teleport anywhere right now, where would it be?" Give fun, unexpected options like "A tropical beach with dancing flamingos," "A cozy mountain cabin with a surprise guest," "A bustling city with hidden treasures," or "An outer space adventure with karaoke." Have participants vote by using creative hand signals or miming their choice, like pretending to sip a coconut drink for the beach or moonwalking for outer space. This playful approach amps up the energy, breaks down barriers, and creates a memorable, interactive moment that gets everyone involved while keeping it light and easy.

Moderate-engagement activities

Moderate-engagement activities are like being in the middle of the pool — deep enough to swim freely but still within reach of the bottom. These activities balance low-key participation with dynamic interaction, providing just the right amount of engagement to keep things interesting without overwhelming anyone. They get people talking, thinking, and connecting at their own pace, building a nice, steady rhythm that keeps the ideas and energy flowing!

Here are a few to get you going:

- **One-to-one**: You and the participant discuss a juicy prompt like "What's one goal lighting you up right now?" Then, take turns diving deep. This back-and-forth turns a simple chat into a meaningful exchange of ideas that elevates the mood.

- **Small group**: Introduce a thought-provoking prompt like "What's one challenge we could totally crush together?" Have everyone pair up and share their thoughts for a few minutes. This gets people talking in a comfortable way, where interaction feels easy and fun.

- **Large group**: Start with a bold question like "What skill or mindset has the power to elevate our industry and take it to the next level?" Then, get the crowd to contribute answers and discuss. It is an instant energy booster that gets everyone in on the action.

High-engagement activities

High-engagement activities are like diving headfirst into the deep end of the pool—they crank up the energy and get everyone all in. These moments push people to think big, share boldly, and dive right into the action. When the room is buzzing with excitement, ideas are flying, connections deepen, and every moment becomes memorable. Whether you're aiming to ignite creativity, encourage collaboration, or drive dynamic discussions, high-engagement activities create the momentum that makes it all happen.

Here are some ways you can kick things up a notch:

- **One-to-one**: Drop a daring prompt like, "What's one big, bold move you've been dying to make but haven't yet?" Then, go all in. Push each other to dig deep, uncover the 'why not?' and turn that big idea into action. It's about creating a super-charged, no-holds-barred conversation that lights a fire under both of you!

- **Small group:** Start the group with a high-energy prompt: "What's the craziest idea we could come up with to solve our biggest challenge?" Then, set a timer and let the ideas fly! Keep the pace quick and the mood light, building on each other's creativity. The goal? Generate as many wild ideas as possible – no judgment, just fun and innovation.

- **Large group:** Kick off with a powerful prompt like, "What's the one thing that would totally transform our results this year?" Invite participants to take turns in the hot seat to share their answers in 30 seconds or less while the rest of the group gives rapid thumbs up or down (physically or electronically) to show agreement or challenge. It's fast, interactive, and elevates the room's energy to 11!

No matter the setting or size of the group, use your powerful prompts as catalysts for change. Decide on the level of engagement you want to create, adapt your approach, and watch how using the energy equation creates a positive shift in the room's atmosphere. It's all about finding that sweet spot of balance and synergy, making every interaction impactful and uplifting.

When you embrace this approach, you're not just boosting your own energy, you're elevating the collective energy and raising the game for everyone around you. By combining powerful prompts with the appropriate level of engagement, you're creating a positive, can-do atmosphere where everyone is fired up, engaged, and ready to achieve impossible goals.

If you're unsure where the individual or group's energy stands, take a step back. Start by tuning into your own energy and syncing up with those around you first. Remember, you can't jump straight to lifting the energy of others (at least not sustainably). You need to tune up and sync up before you can fully step into your role as an energy catalyst and use the right strategy to elevate others.

Key Takeaways

1. Moving from lifting your own energy to lifting others' means building trust and rapport to create space where people feel valued and understood.

2. Improv is not just about wit and laughter; it is a masterclass in the art of dynamic human interaction. Using classic improv principles, you can elevate relational energy, create stronger connections, and lead with a dynamic, collaborative spirit.

3. Approach the energy game from a holistic perspective by understanding the needs of different types of people including Analyzers, Creators, Explorers, and Strategists.

4. The secret to shifting energy in any setting is found in this equation: **Powerful Prompts x Engagement Level = Energy Shift**! A powerful prompt is the fuel, and the level of engagement amplifies the result. The same prompt can create different outcomes in different settings. For low engagement, keep it reflective and calm. For moderate engagement, encourage conversation and collaboration. For high engagement, challenge participants to think big and dive in fully.

Vibe Shifters

Use the following prompts to help put your chapter insights into action.

1. If you could choose a theme song for today, what would it be and why?
2. What's one thing you're excited about right now?
3. Imagine we're all on a mission together — what's the first thing we do?
4. If you could give everyone in this room a superpower, what would it be and why?
5. If you could instantly master one new skill today, what would it be?
6. What's one small win you've had recently that's worth celebrating?
7. If you were given a megaphone to speak to the entire world for one minute, what would you say?
8. If you could trade places with anyone for a day, who would it be and what would you do?
9. If you had to teach a class on one subject right now, what would it be and why?
10. If you had a magic wand to change one thing in the world, what would it be and why?

For additional resources related to engagement, head to kafilondon.com/firedup or scan the QR Code.

PART 3

ENERGY IN ACTION

CHAPTER EIGHT

Energyship

"In an increasingly secular world, our basic needs and desires have not changed. In order for humans to flourish, we need to feel as if something sacred or special is happening in our lives. People still need to feel connected to others!"

- SHIRA GABRIEL, PHD. PROFESSOR,
DEPT OF PSYCHOLOGY, UNIVERSITY OF BUFFALO

Start the ripple

Before we finish up here, let's make sure the idea of leading with energy doesn't just evaporate into thin air as you turn the final pages of this book.

Leadership's true power surge begins when energy drives connections – a dynamic I call…Energyship!

If you have not done so already, jump start your very own ripple by taking a quick energy audit. The audit provides insight into your current energy level based on interactions that shape your daily work and life.

It's an opportunity to discover where you fall on the Energy Ladder of Impact discussed in Chapter 1. Here's a refresh to save you going back to find it!

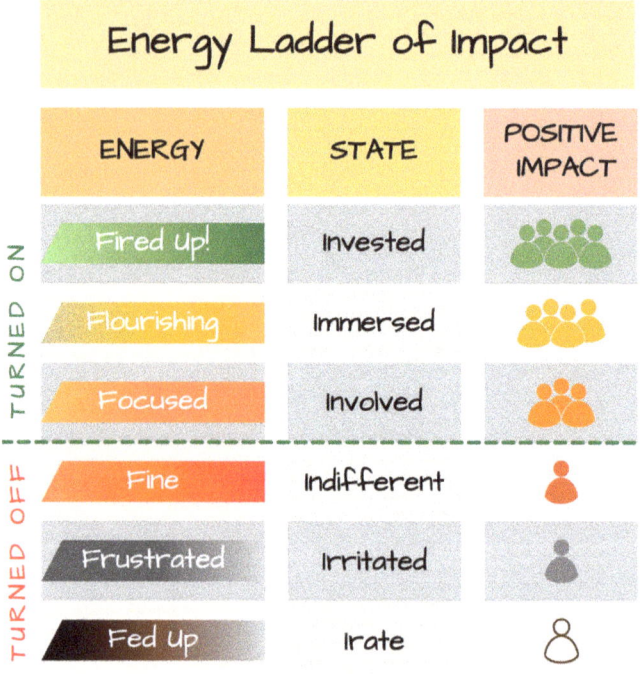

Are you turning up, turned on, and rocking it above the green mid-line (fired up, flourishing, or focused), or are you feeling shut down, stuck below the line (fine, frustrated, or fed up)?

Take charge of your energy by heading to: kafilondon.com/energyaudit and find out where you land on the ladder.

The audit's results will reveal where your energy stands and how you can dial it up to maximize your impact. Remember, every interaction is an opportunity to elevate the energy around you and make a difference.

With your audit results in hand, use the Fired Up! Framework (*Tune Up*, *Sync Up*, and *Lift Up*) and the five igniters (your vitality, vibe, value, voice, and visibility) to optimize your energy.

Ignite Synergy

When your Sparkability Factor is on point, your energy doesn't just stay with you—it ripples out, impacting everyone around you. This is the person-to-people effect we discussed in Chapter 1.

And...when you get a whole crew of people doing the same thing in unison, *Collective Synergy* comes into play.

Collective Synergy is the unstoppable force that happens when individual energies align with others, creating a powerful, unified force that amplifies. The whole team starts working together seamlessly, as personal or "ME" energy transforms into "WE" energy, which lifts the whole group or team.

But it does not stop there!

Collective Effervescence

When synergy energy reaches its peak – it evolves into an ocean of shared energy and unity known as *Collective Effervescence*. You know those moments when you're part of something bigger than yourself, like the indoor cycling class we started with in the introduction? The moments when the room is humming with energy, when everyone's in sync and there is a powerful sense of lifting, unity and excitement. This is where the real magic happens – where the group or team is not just working together, they're vibing on a whole new level, fueling each other's energy and creating something extraordinary - that's Collective Effervescence in action.

I first heard the term Collective Effervescence in the summer of 2023 while attending a week-long workshop at the Baja Campus of Modern Elder Academy. I still remember when our instructor and Founder, Chip Conley, said the magic words in the middle of one of our sessions.

Collective Effervescence.

I discovered sociologist Emile Durkheim coined the term. It describes the intense energy and unity that arises when people come together for a shared experience. It's the electric buzz in the air that lifts everyone up and arises when a group is engaged and energized together creating a deep sense of belonging and connection.[21]

Embrace those shared moments and watch as your interactions build into powerful, uplifting, unifying experiences. Whether in your personal life, professional endeavours, or community activities, harnessing this collective energy will lead to greater connection, innovation, and success.

It's time to tune up, sync up, lift up, and use relational energy and emotional contagion as your tools to create those magical, electrifying moments of Collective Effervescence!

As you close *Fired Up!*, remember your journey does not end here – it's just the beginning. That's right, your journey to leading with energy starts now.

You've uncovered the power of your own energy, learned how to assess the energy of others, and how to lift and shift others. We have also briefly touched on the power of Collective Synergy and

Collective Effervescence. Now it is time to take all that energy, all that insight and unleash it into the world.

You are the spark that can ignite change, the force that can elevate others and the catalyst that can turn ordinary moments into extraordinary experiences. Don't wait for the right moment, create it. Step into every room, every conversation and every interaction with the intention to uplift, connect and inspire. Your energy has the power to shape not just your life, but the lives of those around you.

So, drop the funk, bring the fire and watch the ripples of your impact ignite everything around you!

The ripple starts with you, but the impact? It's bloody limitless!

How can I help?

I truly hope this book gives you the spark, the fuel, and the oxygen to lead with bold, contagious energy and create ripples that change everything, whether it's guiding yourself, uplifting a few, or inspiring a cast of thousands. But I get it – sometimes we need a little extra juice to keep the energy flowing and the ripples spreading. If you or someone in your world could use a partner to keep that fire lit and those ripples rolling, I'd be delighted to help you.

Interactive Keynotes and High-Energy Emceeing

If you want to bring serious energy to your next meeting, event, or conference and create an experience that genuinely captivates, I'm your secret weapon! As an interactive keynoter and energizing emcee, I'm known for bringing the energy! I'll weave compelling stories, thought-provoking questions, and practical insights into engagement opportunities that keep your audience involved and inspired. Together, we'll create unforgettable moments that spark a ripple of enthusiasm and impact, reaching far beyond the event itself. Let's make your event the one everyone talks about.

Corporate Education

Are you ready to take your team's skills, energy, and impact to the next level? My corporate education programs are not your typical training. I bring experiential, high-impact content and engaging delivery, turning learning into an immersive journey. Whether it's leadership development, team dynamics, or fostering a culture of enthusiasm, I'll help your talent tap into their energy, build energy-first connections with team members, and ultimately create ripples of positivity throughout your organization. Let's transform education into empowerment and make learning something your team looks forward to applying – fueling your organization to stand out and gain a competitive edge.

I also offer programming that helps female leaders and executives recalibrate, stand out, and soar – empowering them to break through barriers, own their unique strengths, and lead as authentic, impactful forces.

Mentoring and Executive Coaching

Ready to get your mojo back and lead with more energy? My mentoring and executive coaching programs are designed to help you reignite your spark, build resilience, and prevent burnout. Together, we'll dive deep into strategies to help you replenish your energy, elevate your presence, and become a guiding light for those around you. It's all about cultivating that juicy, person-to-people energy that spreads positivity and impact far and wide. Let's work together to get you back to leading with passion, purpose, and a whole lot of mojo!

HOW CAN I HELP?

Interested in any of these? Email me at hello@kafilondon.com to chat about how we can bring these ideas to life for you or your organization.

Tools for Leading with Energy

Want to elevate the energy in your meetings, workshops, or events? Spark Cards are here to help! This deck of 60 prompts is designed to boost engagement and inspire meaningful conversations—whether you're looking to ignite creativity, foster connections, or create memorable moments that leave everyone feeling energized.

Whether you need a gentle nudge to get things started or a thought-provoking question to spark discussion, these cards are your go-to resource for lifting the vibe in any setting. Ready to transform your interactions?

Learn more or grab a pack at kafilondon.com/sparkcards.

Let's stay connected

I'd love to keep the energy flowing and the conversation going. Sign up for my newsletter, *The Charging Station*, where I share powerful ideas, practical insights, and resources to energize your path forward.

By joining, you'll also get the inside scoop on special content, like tools to spark new thinking or a heads-up about upcoming programs or live experiences. It's my way of staying connected, adding value, and fueling your journey with a bit of extra excitement and momentum.

Stay in touch by signing up for my newsletter, *The Charging Station*, at kafilondon.com.

About the Author

Raised in the UK and now stirring things up state-side, Kafi London has spent over 25 years mastering the people business. She's partnered with top organizations like the Coca-Cola Company, Shell Chemical Company and Hewlett-Packard on global initiatives to elevate their leaders, teams, and talent. Having facilitated hundreds of people-powered experiences, primarily in the US, but also in Europe, she has picked up a simple but powerful fact: people buy your energy before they invest in your thoughts, products, or services.

In today's AI-driven world, where technology is everywhere, our human energy is the juice that genuinely sets us apart. Kafi taps into this wisdom by helping people discover their unique vibe, build authentic connections, and create ripples of impact.

Kafi is a dynamic speaker, author, and engagement strategist who specializes in leading experiences that connect, engage, and energize. Known for her ability to turn any room into a hub of excitement and interaction, Kafi brings her signature blend of fresh ideas, creativity, and high-octane strategies to every session. As your Chief Energy Officer and creator of Spark Cards, Kafi knows how to shake things up and bring serious juice to meetings, events, and conferences.

Her unique approach combines compelling storytelling, interactive activities, and contagious enthusiasm that captivates and motivates. Whether connecting 1:1, leading small groups or large crowds, Kafi delivers the kind of energy that turns ordinary moments into unforgettable experiences, leaving a lasting impact.

Her latest work, *Fired Up! Lead with Energy and Create Ripples of Impact*, offers a practical approach to leading with energy. Kafi is also the co-author of three other books, including 303 Solutions for Communicating Effectively and Getting Results, 303 Solutions for Reaching Goals and Living Your Dreams, and 303 Solutions for Overcoming Challenges, which have empowered countless individuals and organizations to transform their communication, leadership, and team dynamics.

When she's not firing up audiences or leading experiences, you'll find her pushing riders to their limits in a high-energy spin class, tearing up the salsa dance floor with her passion for dance, or flowing through a challenging yoga session. She brings her love for movement and vitality into every aspect of her life, always seeking opportunities to stay active and energized.

Kafi is also passionate about supporting causes close to her heart and actively volunteers in community initiatives like youth mentorship programs and women's empowerment groups, always seeking new ways to connect, inspire, and make a difference that empower others to excel and thrive. The bottom line is that Kafi is about creating meaningful impact and leaving every place and person better than she found them. She has served on the boards of non-profits such as the National Speakers Association, British American Business Council of Georgia, Black Newcomers' Network, and PURE3ON.

Gratitude

This book is a personal achievement that makes me chuckle with nerves, but truthfully, I'm pretty proud of it.

I always tell my clients that it takes courage and spirit to create something and put it out in the world—because the world will judge you! Well, after talking myself out of it for years, I guess it was time to take my own advice. I stand on the shoulders of many individuals and communities who have knowingly and unknowingly contributed to my journey.

I could not have completed *Fired Up!* alone, and I have many people to acknowledge and thank from the bottom of my heart.

Thanks to my editor, Emily Stephenson. Your incredible eye for detail and awesome feedback were game-changers for this book; your guidance really took this project to the next level.

A huge shoutout to the team at Hambone Publishing for making it happen in record time. You guys rock!

To my videographer and photographer, Qiana Avery – thanks for your great work.

To my parents, big sister, brothers, and extended family, thanks for your love and support. To my friends, Chaya, Akunna, Genny, Adrea, Karen and Julie. You have known me the longest and continue to support me through life's highs and lows; thank you for your continued friendship.

To my former boss and friend, Thomas Brown. Thank you for always having my back and believing in me and my ability to deliver excellence, even when I didn't think I had what it took. It has been quite a ride since we met at DA Consulting Group in 1993.

To Ellen Rogin, Mary Kerrigan, Geraldine Ree, Hannah Brown, Lisa Bennett, Winitha Bonney, Chad Littlefield and Emma McQueen – you have all poured into me to bring this book to fruition – thank you!

To Dorothy Andreas, Katherine Johnson, Dr. Patrica Burlaud, Dr. Tara Kenyon, Dana Xavier Dojnik, Martine Resnick, Eileen Lee and Anty Marche for the hours of conversation, support, and accountability we have shared in our quest to live life by design. What a ride it has been and continues to be.

To my state-side mentors: Heather Nicely, Marquel Russell, Rosetta Thurman, Joel Bauer, Jeff St. Laurant, Rich Litvin and Chip Conley. Your programs have continued to guide me over the years.

To my international mentors, Matt Church, Lisa O'Neill, Col Fink, and Christina Joy, thank you for your brilliance, support, and encouragement in getting this book out of my belly and into the world. You have challenged me to get out of my own way, not only to think bigger but to be better, too. Thank you!

I continue to be inspired by my communities and collaborators of big thinkers and doers on a mission to change the world: The

LOLA, PK3 Alpha, Women's Lounge, Strength Sisters, MEA Lighthearted cohort, and PURE3ON. To my Thought Leaders Business School crew, it is a pleasure to ride alongside you. While it continues to be one heck of a journey, our impossible goals are manifesting. I have come to learn that *it just takes time*, so keep going!

To my fitness clients and friends past and present at CycleBar East Cobb, Crunch Fitness, Atlanta Track Club, Solidcore and LA Fitness, who have given me the space and grace to kick their butts on or off the bike over the years – thank you for trusting me.

Last but by no means least, thank you to the many friends, acquaintances, and clients with whom I have had the pleasure of crossing paths in my journey of life. Your light continues to inspire me to keep my light shining and not give up—thank you!

Endnotes

1. Maya Angelou, *The Collected Autobiographies of Maya Angelou* (Modern Library, 2004).

2. Deepak Chopra, *The Seven Spiritual Laws of Success: A Practical Guide to the Fulfillment of Your Dreams* (New World Library, 1994).

3. Richard P Feynman, "Conservation of Energy," in *The Feynman Lectures on Physics. Vol. 1, Chapter 4* (Addison-Wesley, 1963).

4. Ellen Rogin, *Messages from Money* (Two Tango Productions, 2023).

5. Stephen R. Covey, A. Roger Merrill, and Rebecca R. Merrill, *First Things First* (New York: Simon & Schuster, 1994).

6. The Nobel Prize in Chemistry 1997, *NobelPrize.org,* Nobel Media AB, accessed August 23, 2024, https://www.nobelprize.org/prizes/chemistry/1997/summary/.

7. Dalai Lama, commonly attributed.

8. Rob Cross, Wayne Baker, and Andrew Parker, "What Creates Energy in Organizations," *MIT Sloan Management Review*, July 15, 2003.

9. Benjamin P. Owens, Wayne Baker, Randall S. Peterson, and Avery J. Cameron, "*Relational Energy at Work: Implications for Job Engagement and Job Performance,*" Journal of Applied Psychology 100, no. 4 (2015).

10. Emma Seppälä. "*The Best Leaders Have a Contagious Positive Energy,*" Harvard Business Review, April 26, 2022.

11. Luis R. Cortes, "How Relational Energy Impacts Employee Engagement," *Forbes*, April 5, 2023.

12 Mihaly Csikszentmihalyi. *Flow: The Psychology of Optimal Experience* (New York: Harper & Row, 1990).

13 Jim Ziolkowski with James S. Hirsch, *Walk in Their Shoes: Can One Person Change the World?* (New York: Simon & Schuster, 2013).

14 Carol S. Dweck, *Mindset: The New Psychology of Success* (New York: Ballantine Books, 2006).

15 Anna Medaris, "6 Things Researchers Want You to Know About Stress," *American Psychological Association*, accessed July 26, 2024, https://www.apa.org/topics/stress/research-findings.

16 Alexander Eser, "*How Many Words Does a Person Speak on Average per Day?*" *World Metrics*, July 23, 2024, https://worldmetrics.org/average-words-spoken-per-day/.

17 David Kantor, *Reading the Room: Group Dynamics for Coaches and Leaders* (San Francisco: Jossey-Bass, 2012).

18 Vanessa Van Edwards, *Cues: Master the Secret Language of Charismatic Communication* (New York: Penguin Random House, 2022).

19 Gareth Cook, "Why We Are Wired to Connect," *Scientific American*, October 22, 2013.

20 Matt Church, *Amplifiers* (Wrightbooks, 2013).

21 Émile Durkheim, *The Elementary Forms of Religious Life*, trans. Karen E. Fields (New York: The Free Press, 1995).

Books Referenced

Cook, Gareth. "Why We Are Wired to Connect." Scientific American, October 22, 2013. https://www.scientificamerican.com/article/why-we-are-wired-to-connect/.

Van Edwards, Vanessa. *Cues: Master the Secret Language of Charismatic Communication.* New York: Penguin Random House, 2022.

Kantor, David. *Reading the Room: Group Dynamics for Coaches and Leaders.* San Francisco: Jossey-Bass, 2012.

Smith, Paul. *The 10 Stories Great Leaders Tell.* Naperville: Simple Truths, 2019.

Webster, Tamsen. *Find Your Red Thread: Make Your Big Ideas Irresistible.* Victoria: Page Two, 2021.

Lim, Jenn. *Beyond Happiness: How Authentic Leaders Prioritize Purpose and People for Growth and Impact.* New York: Grand Central Publishing, 2021.

Church, Matt, Peter Cook, and Scott Stein. *The Thought Leaders Practice: Do Work You Love with People You Like the Way You Want.* Melbourne: Thought Leaders, 2015.

Schaefer, Mark W. *KNOWN: The Handbook for Building and Unleashing Your Personal Brand in the Digital Age.* Tennessee: Schaefer Marketing Solutions, 2017.

Giles, Sunnie. "The Most Important Leadership Competencies, According to Leaders Around the World." *Harvard Business Review*, March 15, 2016. https://hbr.org/2016/03/the-most-important-leadership-competencies-according-to-leaders-around-the-world.

Seymour, Laurie. "Is it Charisma? Or Essence? Why the Difference is Important." The Baca Institute. Accessed July 26, 2024. https://thebacainstitute.com/charisma-essence/

www.ingramcontent.com/pod-product-compliance
Lightning Source LLC
Chambersburg PA
CBHW041307110526
44590CB00028B/4271